T0361288

Cambridge Elements ≡

Elements in Metaphysics
edited by
Tuomas E. Tahko
University of Bristol

IDENTITY

Erica Shumener
Syracuse University

Shaftesbury Road, Cambridge CB2 8EA, United Kingdom

One Liberty Plaza, 20th Floor, New York, NY 10006, USA

477 Williamstown Road, Port Melbourne, VIC 3207, Australia

314–321, 3rd Floor, Plot 3, Splendor Forum, Jasola District Centre, New Delhi – 110025, India

103 Penang Road, #05–06/07, Visioncrest Commercial, Singapore 238467

Cambridge University Press is part of Cambridge University Press & Assessment, a department of the University of Cambridge.

We share the University's mission to contribute to society through the pursuit of education, learning and research at the highest international levels of excellence.

www.cambridge.org
Information on this title: www.cambridge.org/9781009001342

DOI: 10.1017/9781009004671

First published 2022

A catalogue record for this publication is available from the British Library.

ISBN 978-1-009-00134-2 Paperback
ISSN 2633-9862 (online)
ISSN 2633-9854 (print)

Identity

Elements in Metaphysics

DOI: 10.1017/9781009004671
First published online: September 2022

Erica Shumener
Syracuse University

Author for correspondence: Erica Shumener, ericashumener@gmail.com

Abstract: Identity criteria are powerful tools for the metaphysician. They tell us when items are identical or distinct. Some varieties of identity criteria also try to explain in virtue of what items are identical or distinct. This Element has two objectives: to discuss formulations of identity criteria and to take a closer look at one notorious criterion of object identity, Leibniz's Law. The first section concerns the form of identity criteria. The second section concerns the better-regarded half of Leibniz's Law, the indiscernibility of identicals. The third section turns to the more controversial half of Leibniz's Law, the identity of indiscernibles. The author considers alternatives to Leibniz's Law as well as the possibility that there are no adequate identity criteria to be found.

Keywords: identity, identity criteria, metaphysics, Leibniz's Law, objects

ISBNs: 9781009001342 (PB), 9781009004671 (OC)
ISSNs: 2633-9862 (online), 2633-9854 (print)

Contents

1 Identity Criteria   1

2 The Indiscernibility of Identicals   17

3 The Identity of Indiscernibles   31

4 Counterexamples to the Identity of Indiscernibles
   and Alternatives to Leibniz's Law   40

5 Concluding Remarks   51

   References   52

1 Identity Criteria

1.1 What Are Identity Criteria and Why Should We Care about Them?

Here are some examples of identity criteria:

- Object x is identical with object y just in case x and y have all the same properties.
- Sets A and B are identical if and only if A and B share all and only the same members.
- Events x and y are identical if and only if they are comprised of the same subjects, properties (and relations), and time intervals.
- Person x at t is identical with person y at t′ if and only if y at t′ is psychologically continuous with x at t′.

Identity criteria are powerful tools for the metaphysician. Equipped with identity criteria, theories gain predictive power. Suppose we had a comprehensive identity criterion that tells us when a person at one spatiotemporal location is identical with a person at another spatiotemporal location. Such a criterion will tell us whether individual identity and distinctness claims – such as "Mark Twain in 1860 = Samuel Clemens in 1875" and "Mark Twain in 1860 ≠ Harriet Tubman in 1854" – are true or not. We could also use it to answer questions like these:

- Will Cora survive the transition from being a rebellious, skateboarding seventeen-year-old to being a conservative forty-five-year-old investment banker?
- Will Harry survive a trip through a teletransporter that disassembles and then reassembles his physical matter?

An identity criterion for personal identity would tell us which changes we would survive and which changes would kill us. Likewise, identity criteria for events, facts, properties, material objects, actions, and objects in general would determine whether entities in those categories are identical or distinct under various circumstances.

Identity criteria can also help us shed light on our inferences involving identity claims. For instance, we know that the American author Mark Twain has an acerbic sense of humor. When we learn that Mark Twain is identical with Samuel Clemens ("Mark Twain" is Clemens' pen name), we attribute that acerbic sense of humor to Samuel Clemens. Although that inference seems obvious, we may wonder what principle(s) license it. Identity criteria, such as Leibniz's Law, can answer that question. Leibniz's Law, named after Gottfried Wilhelm von Leibniz, states – roughly – that individuals are identical if and only if they share their properties. If Mark Twain has the property of *possessing an acerbic sense of humor*, then Leibniz's Law tells us that if Mark Twain = Samuel Clemens, then Samuel Clemens has that same property.

Although an identity criterion like Leibniz's Law helps license plausible inferences, it can also be a source of mystery. While it is controversial whether humans can survive trips through teleporters, most of us agree that a person can survive the loss of a single strand of hair. But suppose that Amelia loses a single strand of hair at 12 p.m. on Tuesday. Amelia at 11:59 a.m. has 100,000 strands of hair while Amelia at 12:01 p.m. has 99,999 strands of hair. Prima facie, 11:59 Amelia possesses a property (*100,000 strands of hair*) that 12:01 Amelia lacks. Leibniz's Law seems to tell us that 11:59 Amelia is distinct from 12:01 Amelia, contrary to our initial judgment that Amelia survives losing a strand of hair.

This Element has two objectives: to discuss formulations of identity criteria and to take a closer look at Leibniz's Law. The first section concerns the general form of identity criteria. I address varieties of identity criteria present in the metaphysics literature and compare them. After providing an overview of varieties of identity criteria, I turn to a focused discussion of Leibniz's Law. Leibniz's Law is a conjunction of two principles of object individuation, the indiscernibility of identicals and the identity of indiscernibles. The second section concerns the better-regarded half of Leibniz's Law, the indiscernibility of identicals. The indiscernibility of identicals states that *if* objects x and y are identical, then x and y share their features. This principle seems so obvious to some that it even strikes them as akin to a logical truth. After all, if x and y are numerically one and the same object, that object must have all the same properties as itself. How can an object have different properties from the ones it itself has? Nevertheless, as we witnessed in the previous paragraph, there are challenges to the indiscernibility of identicals, and I will explain how they arise. In the third section, I turn to the more controversial half of Leibniz's Law, the identity of indiscernibles. The identity of indiscernibles states that if objects x and y share all the same properties, they are identical. This principle, depending on how it is interpreted, is less obvious. Why could there not be distinct objects – spheres, eggs, subatomic particles, or what have you – that share their features? We can imagine two eggs that have the same shape, size, color, and density along with the rest of their characteristics, can we not? I will explore alleged counterexamples to the identity of indiscernibles as well as alternative principles of object individuation that may serve as attractive competitors to the identity of indiscernibles. Finally, I will consider the possibility that there are no adequate criteria for object identity to be found.

1.2 Varieties of Identity Criteria

1.2.1 Material and the Modal Identity Criteria

At the most basic level, an identity criterion tells us when entities are numerically identical or distinct. There are many ways to formulate identity criteria, and I will examine some of their variations. First, I focus on the modal strength of identity criteria. Let us consider Leibniz's Law, the identity criterion that will be the subject of focus in the following sections. Here is one standard formulation of an identity criterion using Leibniz's Law:

Material Leibniz's Law: $\forall x \forall y (x = y \equiv \forall P(Px \equiv Py))$

This criterion provides necessary and sufficient conditions for the identity of individuals x and y: x and y are identical just in case they share all their properties. The x- and y-quantifiers range over objects, while the P-quantifier ranges over monadic properties. We will plausibly need to restrict the P-quantifier so that it does not range over *all* monadic properties. I will leave such restrictions to the next two sections.

Material Leibniz's Law is an *extensional* or "material"[1] identity criterion: it only provides a criterion for identity and distinctness for entities in the actual world; hence, we call it "Material Leibniz's Law." We can contrast this with a modalized version of Leibniz's Law, which is an instance of a Modal Identity Criterion:

Modal Leibniz's Law: $\square \forall x \forall y (x = y \equiv \forall P(Px \equiv Py))$

Modal Leibniz's Law states that, necessarily, x is identical with y if and only if x and y share all their properties. Material identity criteria lack this modal strength. Material Leibniz's Law holds when all distinct objects differ with respect to at least one property at the actual world, and all identical objects do not differ with respect to any of their properties at the actual world. Certain popular counterexamples to Modal Leibniz's Law will not impact Material Leibniz's Law as long as those counterexamples do not describe actual states of affairs.

One popular counterexample to a version of Leibniz's Law is Max Black's sphere world (Black 1952). Black imagines a universe containing only two spheres with the same shape, mass, color, and all other physical characteristics. Let us suppose that the spheres reside five meters apart. The spheres are called "Castor" and "Pollux." Presumably, Castor and Pollux share all their qualitative properties (more on this notion in Section 3) even though they are distinct. One

---

[1] See Fine (2016).

may attempt to distinguish the spheres on the basis of their locational properties, but Black doubts this would work. If we maintain that Castor is distinct from Pollux because Castor has the property *located at spacetime region a* and Pollux has the property *located at spacetime region b*, then this only pushes the problem back: how can we distinguish between spacetime region a and spacetime region b? Do these regions not share all *their* properties?

Black's case challenges Modal Leibniz's Law, which states that, necessarily, if x and y are distinct, they differ with respect to their properties. If this is a metaphysically possible scenario in which distinct objects share all their properties, Modal Leibniz's Law must be false. While such a case may present a counterexample to Modal Leibniz's Law, it will not present a counterexample to Material Leibniz's Law because the actual world is not one that contains only two spheres floating in empty space.

It is somewhat difficult to find pressing counterexamples to Material Leibniz's Law. Because the universe does not appear to involve a symmetrical distribution of matter, we should often be able to distinguish actual objects by the different relational properties they have. Even if we have two duplicate spheres, Actual Castor and Actual Pollux in the actual world, we could find relational properties to distinguish them. For instance, suppose Actual Castor and Actual Pollux materialized in the state of Alabama. Figure 1 shows a map of where they materialized.

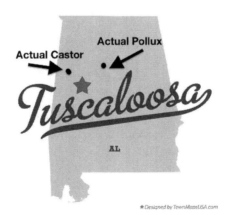

Figure 1 Map of the locations of Actual Castor and Actual Pollux in Alabama. The map is a modified version of the map of Tuscaloosa, Alabama, found on TownmapsUSA.com. I have added the dots, names, and arrows used to represent Actual Castor and Actual Pollux. License for use: https://creativecommons.org/licenses/by-nc/3.0/

Given their locations, we can see that Actual Castor and Actual Pollux differ in their distance from Tuscaloosa. Actual Castor and Actual Pollux differ with respect to the following properties: Actual Castor is 50 miles from Tuscaloosa. Actual Pollux is not. Actual Pollux is 100 miles from Tuscaloosa. So even though Actual Castor and Actual Pollux may be indistinguishable with respect to their mass, temperature, shape, color, and so on, we can distinguish them by their relational properties. Furthermore, there are many related properties that will distinguish Actual Castor and Actual Pollux. It just so happens that the Alabama Museum of Natural History (located in Tuscaloosa) contains an intact skull of an American Mastodon. Actual Castor has the property of *being 50 miles from the skull of a mastodon*, while Actual Pollux lacks this property and instead has the property *being 100 miles from the skull of a mastodon*. The existence of Actual Castor and Actual Pollux does not pose a counterexample to Material Leibniz's Law.

This is not to say that we cannot find counterexamples to Material Leibniz's Law (see Section 3 for further discussion of this), but potential counterexamples to Modal Leibniz's Law will not immediately serve as counterexamples to material versions. I have been discussing Leibniz's Law specifically, but this lesson should apply to formulations of identity criteria in general. Material versions of identity criteria are weaker than their necessitated counterparts, and it is easier to find potential counterexamples to the modal versions than it is to the material ones.

Greater resistance to counterexamples provides a prima facie reason to favor material identity criteria over modal identity criteria. But there are costs to embracing material identity criteria over modal ones. Let us return to the case of Leibniz's Law. If we adopt Material Leibniz's Law instead of Modal Leibniz's Law, we face the question of why this identity criterion is only contingently true.

Some philosophers have proposed that at least certain identity claims of the form "x = y" are necessarily true if true. I am thinking specifically of philosophers such as Saul Kripke (1980), who believe that when identity claims include proper names flanking the two sides of the identity predicate the claim is necessarily true. For Kripke, proper names (like "Mark Twain") refer to the same individual in every possible world in which the individual exists. They are "rigid designators" in his terminology. If "Mark Twain" and "Samuel Clemens" refer to the same individual in the actual world, they do so in every possible world. Accordingly, the identity claim "Mark Twain = Samuel Clemens" is true in every possible world if it is true in the actual world. It would be surprising for certain identity and distinctness facts involving individuals to obtain necessarily even though the identity criteria for such individuals do not obtain necessarily.

Relatedly, whether we will be satisfied with material identity criteria depends on what we want to use the identity criteria for. Often, we ask questions like: Were I to lose half of my brain in an accident would I be numerically one and the same person? Were this set to contain an extra member, would it be the same set? And, if some event had taken place earlier would it have been the same event? These questions concern counterfactual circumstances. If our identity criteria are to be useful in answering these questions, we would expect them to be *modally stable* – true in at least the other possible worlds we are concerned with when asking these questions. For these reasons, we may search for modal identity criteria rather than material ones. These are not conclusive reasons to adopt a modal identity criterion over a material one. My intention is merely to highlight some issues that arise when opting for one type of identity criterion over the other.

Modal identity criteria have a necessity operator appearing with wide scope, but there are varieties of necessity operators. Modal identity criteria can come in different strengths, depending on what notion of necessity we deploy. We may maintain that the biconditional holds with metaphysical necessity or rather with physical necessity. In the former case, the identity criterion is supposed to hold in every metaphysically possible world. In the latter case, the biconditional would hold in every possible world that is consistent with the actual laws of nature.[2] In metaphysical discussions of identity criteria, philosophers often have the metaphysical rather than the physical or nomological necessity operator in mind.

1.2.2 Explanatory Identity Criteria

We can also distinguish between *explanatory* and *nonexplanatory* identity criteria. Explanatory identity criteria do not provide necessary and sufficient conditions for identity and distinctness – at least not directly. Instead, they tell us *in virtue of what* identity and distinctness facts hold. In recent years, explanatory identity criteria have taken the form of grounding criteria for identity and distinctness.[3] We can understand the *in virtue of* relation in terms of ground. We can convert the previous modal and material identity criteria for set identity and Leibniz's Law to explanatory identity criteria as follows:

---

[2] I will speak of different metaphysical possibilities as different metaphysically possible worlds, but nothing I say should hinge on adopting a possible worlds framework as opposed to another framework about modality.

[3] See Burgess (2012), Fine (2016), Shumener (2020a; 2020b), and Wörner (2021).

Explanatory Set Identity:

If set x = set y then x = y is fully grounded in the fact ∀s (s is a member of
x ≡ s is a member of y)

If set x ≠ set y then x ≠ y is fully grounded in the fact ∃s ((s is a member of
x ∨ s is a member of y) & ~(s is a member of x & s is a member of y)).

Explanatory Leibniz's Law:[4]

If x = y then x = y is fully grounded in the fact ∀P(Px ≡ Py)

If x ≠ y then x ≠ y is fully grounded in the fact ∃P((Px ∨ Py) & ∼ (Px & Py)).

What is ground? The notion of ground has been popularized over the past
decade by many philosophers.[5] Metaphysicians typically understand ground
as either a relation (holding among facts) or a sentential operator. When
x grounds y, y holds in virtue of x. Ground is supposed to be either a type of
metaphysical explanation or a relation that backs metaphysical explanation,
depending on which grounding theorists one consults.[6] When a fact is
ungrounded, it is not grounded by any further facts. I take ungrounded facts to
be metaphysically fundamental.

There are many contexts in which we want to claim that certain facts hold in
virtue of other facts. For example, we want to determine whether:

- normative facts obtain in virtue of descriptive ones (e.g., does "Action x is
  morally required" hold in virtue of "Action x maximizes happiness"?)
- mental facts obtain in virtue of physical facts (e.g., does "s is in pain" hold in
  virtue of "s's c-fibers are firing"?)
- determinable facts obtain in virtue of determinate facts (e.g., does "Annie's
  shirt is red" hold in virtue of "Annie's shirt is scarlet"?)
- disjunctive facts obtain in virtue of their disjuncts (e.g., does "Either
  Pittsburgh is in Kentucky or Pittsburgh is in Pennsylvania" hold in virtue of
  "Pittsburgh is in Pennsylvania"?).

Grounding theorists often propose that the same notion of *in virtue of* appears in
these sentences, and we can formulate the corresponding claims in terms of ground.

- "Action x is morally required" is fully grounded in "Action x maximizes
  happiness."

---

[4] Technically, this is an explanatory version of only one half of Leibniz's Law, the identity of
indiscernibles. We discuss this issue in Section 3.

[5] See Fine (2001; 2012), Schaffer (2009), Rosen (2010), Raven (2013; 2015), as well as many
others.

[6] See Trogdon (2013), Thompson (2016), Maurin (2019), and Glazier (2020) for discussion of the
relationship between ground and metaphysical explanation.

- "s is in pain" is fully grounded in "s's c-fibers are firing."
- "Annie's shirt is red" is fully grounded in "Annie's shirt is scarlet."
- "Either Pittsburgh is in Kentucky or Pittsburgh is in Pennsylvania" is fully grounded in "Pittsburgh is in Pennsylvania."

We may also accept general grounding principles concerning the facts in question: normative facts, in general, hold in virtue of descriptive facts in the sense that they are grounded in descriptive facts. If we agree with grounding theorists at this juncture, we may suppose that certain *in virtue of* claims hold for identity and distinctness facts as well, and that these claims should be understood in terms of ground. For instance, we may be inclined to accept:

- The fact that individual x is identical with individual y obtains in virtue of the fact that x and y share all their properties.
- Set x is identical with set y in virtue of the fact that x and y share all their members.
- Person x at t is identical with person y at t′ in virtue of the fact that y at t′ is psychologically continuous with x at t.

If these are statements of ground, then that suggests we will uphold explanatory identity criteria; perhaps there is a general principle (or set of general principles) telling us how identity and distinctness facts are grounded. In what follows, we appeal to a grounding relation that holds among facts.[7] A fact is grounded by another fact or a plurality of facts. We can also distinguish between full and partial ground. I take full ground to be a primitive notion. But intuitively, P fully grounds Q when Q holds in virtue of P and P is sufficient on its own to explain Q. P partially grounds Q when P on its own or together with further facts fully grounds Q. For instance, the fact that the scarf is scarlet *fully grounds* the fact that the scarf is red. The former fact suffices to ground the latter. But the fact that the sky is blue only partly grounds the conjunctive fact that the sky is blue and the grass is green. That conjunctive fact is fully grounded in the plurality of facts: the sky is blue, the grass is green.

Where P, Q, and R are facts, both full and partial ground should obey the following conditions:

Asymmetry: If P grounds Q, then Q does not ground P.

Transitivity: If P grounds Q and Q grounds R, then P grounds R.

---

[7] Some grounding theorists take ground to be a sentential operator rather than a relation holding between facts. See Fine (2012).

Irreflexivity: P does not ground P.

Grounding Necessitation: If P fully grounds Q then necessarily, if P then Q.

While these are popular constraints of ground, all of these constraints have been questioned or rejected by at least some philosophers working on ground.[8] Nevertheless, we will assume these constraints hold for now – this will allow us to get a better grasp of how we can deploy a mainstream conception of ground to understand identity criteria.

Now we have the basic understanding of the notion of ground – of the relation appealed to in explanatory identity criteria – I will highlight some ways in which explanatory identity criteria differ from modal and material identity criteria. Modal and material identity criteria do not entail corresponding explanatory identity criteria. For example, Material Leibniz's Law does not necessitate an explanatory relationship in either direction. We cannot conclude from Material Leibniz's Law that objects' having the same properties explains their identity. We also cannot infer from Material Leibniz's Law that the identity of objects x and y explains the fact that x and y share all their properties. Material Leibniz's Law only tells us that objects have the same properties *if and only if* they are identical. Modal Leibniz's Law does not entail corresponding explanatory identity criteria either. Even if it is metaphysically necessary that x = y if and only if x and y share all the same properties, we cannot, on that basis, conclude either (a) that x and y's sharing their properties explains x = y or (b) the fact that x = y explains x and y's sharing their properties.

It is compatible with modal and material identity criteria that no explanatory relationship holds whatsoever. The choice of whether to adopt explanatory identity criteria rather than (or in addition to) modal or material identity criteria will depend upon one's explanatory ambitions when advancing identity criteria. Why would one wish to defend explanatory identity criteria? If we think that, when providing identity criteria, we are stating *in virtue of what* identity and distinctness facts hold, and we take the *in virtue of* relation to be asymmetric, then this motivates an appeal to explanatory identity criteria.

We may be attempting to uncover this *in virtue of* relationship when we attend to various identity-related puzzles. When considering whether a person x entering a Star Trek–style transporter device is numerically identical with a person y who emerges from a Star Trek–style transporter device at a later time, we do not merely want to know whether x and y are numerically identical or

---

[8] For someone who questions asymmetry, see Koslicki (2015). For those who develop reflexive accounts of ground (often called "weak ground"), see Fine (2012) and deRosset (2013). For rejecting transitivity, see Schaffer (2012), and see Skiles (2015) for a rejection of grounding necessitation.

distinct, but also in virtue of what their identity or distinctness holds. Likewise, it would not be enough – some philosophers think – to establish that Castor and Pollux are distinct yet qualitatively indiscernible spheres, ones that share their mass, shape, density, temperature, color, and so on. We also want to know *why* Castor and Pollux are distinct, given that they are qualitatively indiscernible.

Not everyone is interested in this explanatory project when investigating identity criteria. There are some potential reasons to accept modal or material identity criteria and reject explanatory identity criteria. First, one may be skeptical of notions of metaphysical explanation or ground in general.[9] If we understand metaphysical explanation in terms of ground, and one is skeptical about ground, then one will deny that there are identity criteria that tell us how identity and distinctness facts are grounded.

But even if one accepts that some facts are metaphysically explained or grounded, one can deny that we need explanatory identity criteria. If identity and distinctness facts (at least some of them) are good candidates for fundamental facts, then it is not clear that we need explanatory identity criteria. One thought is that the identity relation is a primitive, logical notion, and perhaps some facts involving primitive logical relations need no explanation. Williamson (1990: 145) echoes the idea that identity facts do not need to be explained. He maintains that for any objects belonging to a kind F, we should not try to explain why they are identical. David Lewis (1986: 192–93) also claimed that "there is never any problem about what makes something identical to itself." Neither Lewis nor Williamson had notions of ground explicitly in mind in these passages, but if we are sympathetic to their claims, we may resist attempts to provide explanatory identity criteria.[10]

Another related reason to deny the existence of explanatory identity criteria is to claim that identity and distinctness facts are not explained; rather, they do the explaining.[11] For instance, identity and distinctness facts are not explained by objects sharing or differing in their properties; instead, the identity and distinctness of objects explain their sharing or differing in properties. In this case, the explanatory relation would point in the opposite direction from the direction it points in in the explanatory identity criteria listed earlier: identity and distinctness facts do not stand in need of explanation. They explain other facts. As such, we should deny the need for explanatory identity criteria here as well. If the identity and distinctness facts have this kind of explanatory power, we could treat such

---

[9] See Wilson (2014) and Koslicki (2015) for skepticism about ground.

[10] Also see Bueno (2014) for considerations in favor of taking identity to be fundamental.

[11] See Wilhelm (2021) for a fascinating discussion of the explanatory power of identity facts.

facts as explanatory bedrock, primitive facts that explain various features of the objects or entities appearing in them. I will further explore the idea that identity and distinctness facts are primitive or unexplained in Section 4.

We have now seen how explanatory identity criteria differ from modal and material identity criteria. We can accept material and modal criteria without accepting corresponding explanatory identity criteria. But can we accept explanatory identity criteria without accepting the corresponding modal or material identity criteria? Matters are more complicated here. Let us focus on Explanatory Leibniz's Law:

Explanatory Leibniz's Law:

> If $x = y$ then $x = y$ is fully grounded in the fact $\forall P(Px \equiv Py)$
> If $x \neq y$ then $x \neq y$ is fully grounded in the fact $\exists P((Px \lor Py) \& \sim (Px \& Py))$.[12]

If we interpret the conditional formulations of both clauses of Explanatory Leibniz's Law to be material conditionals, then the explanatory identity criterion only tells us how identity and distinctness facts are grounded in the actual world. If so, then Explanatory Leibniz's Law does not generate a corresponding modal identity criterion. For all Explanatory Leibniz's Law says, there are identity and distinctness facts in other possible worlds that are not grounded in $\forall P(Px \equiv Py)$ or in $\exists P((Px \lor Py) \& \sim (Px \& Py))$. But there is nothing stopping us from reformulating explanatory identity criteria so that they have modal strength built in explicitly.[13]

Do explanatory identity criteria entail material identity criteria? Let us take a closer look at Explanatory and Material Leibniz's Law. Material Leibniz's Law states that $x = y \equiv \forall P(Px \equiv Py)$. In other words, if $x = y$ then $\forall P(Px \equiv Py)$, and if $\forall P(Px \equiv Py)$ then $x = y$. Explanatory Leibniz's Law will entail both conditionals, given certain plausible assumptions. Due to the first clause of Explanatory Leibniz's Law, we know that if $x = y$, $x = y$ is grounded in $\forall P(Px \equiv Py)$. Furthermore, it is plausible to assume that if P grounds Q, P obtains. This follows from a factive conception of ground, which states that

---

[12] I remain neutral as to whether to formulate Explanatory Leibniz's Law generally or generically. See Section 1.2.3 for discussion.

[13] For instance, perhaps we can adopt the following:

Modal Explanatory Leibniz's Law:
> Necessarily, if $x = y$ then $x = y$ is fully grounded in the fact $\forall P(Px \equiv Py)$
> Necessarily, if $x \neq y$ then $x \neq y$ is fully grounded in the fact $\exists P((Px \lor Py) \& \sim (Px \& Py))$.

if P grounds Q, P and Q obtain. So if x = y obtains, and x = y is grounded in $\forall P(Px \equiv Py)$, then it follows that $\forall P(Px \equiv Py)$ obtains.

What about the other conditional, if $\forall P(Px \equiv Py)$, then x = y? Let us consider the contrapositive of the conditional: if x ≠ y, then $\sim \forall P(Px \equiv Py)$. This conditional will follow straightforwardly from Explanatory Leibniz's Law. We can establish this conditional using the second clause of Explanatory Leibniz's Law. If x ≠ y, then x ≠ y is grounded in $\sim \forall P(Px \equiv Py)$. We then know, by the factivity of ground, $\sim \forall P(Px \equiv Py)$ must obtain. Thus, if x ≠ y, then $\sim \forall P(Px \equiv Py)$. Equivalently, if $\forall P(Px \equiv Py)$, then x = y. As long as we deploy a factive conception of ground, we can retrieve Material Leibniz's Law from Explanatory Leibniz's Law.

1.2.3 Definitional Identity Criteria

Another thought is that at least some identity criteria are, in some sense, *definitional*. Rather than providing metaphysical explanations for x's being identical with y or x's being distinct from y, identity criteria may offer something akin to a definition of x's being identical with y. A related idea is that identity criteria are, or at least can be, analytically true.

This line of thought appears in the discussion of Hume's Principle in the philosophy of mathematics. Hume's Principle is that the number of Fs is the same as the number of Gs just in case there exists a one-to-one correspondence between the Fs and the Gs. Hume's Principle potentially offers an identity criterion for "the number of Xs." Following Ted Sider's (2007) formulation, Hume's Principle takes the logical form of a material identity criterion in our parlance:

Hume's Principle: $\forall F \forall G(\#x{:}Fx = \#x{:}Gx \equiv Eq(F, G))$

Or, "the number of Fs = the number of Gs iff F and G are equinumerous." It is contested whether Hume's Principle is an analytic truth and whether Hume's Principle provides an implicit definition of either "the number of Xs" or "the number of Fs = the number of Gs." To see why this is a locus of debate, we must look to the history of Hume's Principle. While named after David Hume,[14] Gottlob Frege brought Hume's Principle to the forefront of discussion in his *The Foundations of Arithmetic (Die Grundlagen der Arithmetik)*.[15]

---

[14] Hume states: "When two numbers are so combined, as that the one has always an unite answering to every unite of the other, we pronounce them equal; and it is for want of such a standard of equality in extension, that geometry can scarce be esteemed a perfect and infallible science" (Hume 2007: 51).

[15] See Lowe (1989) for discussion of Frege's contributions to the notion of an identity criterion.

Frege wished to derive the principles of arithmetic from principles of logic and logical concepts – the primary objective of the logicist program of the late nineteenth and early twentieth centuries. In Frege's *Begriffsschrift* and *Grundlagen*, Frege developed many of the tools and ideas he would later use in his later work *The Basic Laws of Arithmetic* (*Grundgesetze der Arithmetik*) to derive the principles of arithmetic from a second-order predicate calculus along with certain basic axioms.

In the *Grundlagen*, Frege considers adopting Hume's Principle as an axiom, but he ultimately rejects doing so.[16] The reasons why Frege rejects taking Hume's Principle as an axiom are complex.[17] What is important for our purposes is that Frege provides an alternative definition of "the number of Xs," and this alternative definition requires Frege to posit an axiom called "Basic Law V." Bertrand Russell famously demonstrated that Frege's system leads to paradox ("Russell's Paradox"). And Basic Law V is typically recognized as the culpable source of the paradox. Russell's Paradox eventually caused Frege to abandon his logicist project of deriving the principles of arithmetic from the principles of logic.

Later in the twentieth century, philosophers recognized that Frege's derivations of principles of arithmetic from principles of logic could proceed without Basic Law V as long as we take Hume's Principle as an axiom (*contra* Frege).[18] This revived debate among the "Neo-Fregeans" about whether Hume's Principle could, despite what Frege thought, be an analytic truth and provide a definition of "the number of Xs." If we take Hume's Principle to be an axiom, perhaps a version of Frege's program can succeed.

It would take us too far afield to enter into the details of Neo-Fregeanism. What we should recognize is that some philosophers may see Hume's Principle – and perhaps other identity criteria as well – as providing implicit definitions. If we want to make this definitional character explicit, that would give rise to identity criteria taking a novel form. For instance, if we want a definitional version of Leibniz's Law – perhaps in addition to Material Leibniz's Law – we could posit:

Definitional Leibniz's Law: $\forall x \forall y (x = y =_{df} \forall P(Px \equiv Py))$

Instead of stating a universally quantified biconditional, Definitional Leibniz's Law states a universally quantified definitional claim: for any objects x and y, we define " x = y" as "x and y share all and only the same properties." Positing definitional identity criteria raises interesting questions and issues. Are

---

[16] See Frege (1980 [1884]: section 66).

[17] See Heck (1997) for a helpful discussion of Frege's "Julius Caesar objection" to Hume's Principle.

[18] See Parsons (1965) and Wright (1983) among others.

definitional identity criteria replacements for explanatory identity criteria, or are definitional and explanatory identity criteria compatible? For which types of entities (numbers, sets, people, material objects, etc.) is it appropriate to posit definitional identity criteria? When we have competing identity criteria, how do we adjudicate whether one identity criterion provides a better definition than another? And so on. In what follows, we will constrain the discussion to material, modal, and explanatory identity criteria. Those interested in questions surrounding definitional identity criteria are encouraged to consult the literature on Neo-Fregeanism in the philosophy of math.[19]

1.2.4 General versus Generic Identity Criteria

I have examined four varieties of identity criteria so far: modal, material, explanatory, and definitional identity criteria. But there are other dimensions of variation among identity criteria. Fine (2016) distinguishes between general and generic identity criteria. General identity criteria are formulated using universal generalizations. They tell us that for *any* objects or entities x and y, x = y holds when some condition holds. We can advance general explanatory identity criteria, general modal identity criteria, or general material identity criteria. Here are two examples of general identity criteria:

General Material Leibniz's Law: $\forall x \forall y(x = y \equiv \forall P(Px \equiv Py))$

General Explanatory Set-Identity:

$\forall x \forall y$ (Set(x) & Set(y) & x = y $\supset$ (x = y is fully grounded in $\forall z(z \in x \equiv z \in y)))$
 $\forall x \forall y$ (Set(x) & Set(y) & x $\neq$ y $\supset$ (x $\neq$ y is fully grounded in the fact $\exists s$ ((s is a member of x or s is a member of y) & $\sim$ (s is a member of x and s is a member of y)))).

These two identity criteria have in common that they utilize universal generalizations ranging over the objects in question. Fine characterizes general identity criteria as follows: "[The general criterion] tells us, for any two particular objects of the sort in question, what makes them the same" (Fine, 2016: 4). We can use general identity criteria to straightforwardly tell us about individual identity and distinctness facts, that is, those involving individual objects. If we accept the general version of Material Leibniz's Law, we can determine whether individual objects are identical or distinct. Mark Twain is identical with Samuel

---

[19] In addition to Parsons (1965), Wright (1983), Heck (1997), and Sider (2007), see, for example, Boolos (1997), Wright and Hale (2001), and Donaldson (2017).

Clemens just in case they share all and only the same properties. And Genghis Khan is distinct from Napoleon just in case there is some property that one of them has and the other lacks. These claims are instances of (or entailed by instances of) General Material Leibniz's Law.

Likewise, if we accept a general version of Explanatory Set Identity, then, presumably, we can identify the grounds of an identity fact like {Socrates} = {Socrates}. This is because the fact "{Socrates} = {Socrates} $\supset$ ({Socrates} = {Socrates} is fully grounded in $\forall z(z \in$ {Socrates} $\equiv z \in$ {Socrates})))" is an instance of General Explanatory Set Identity. Thus, the grounding fact "({Socrates} = {Socrates} is fully grounded in $\forall z(z \in$ {Socrates} $\equiv z \in$ {Socrates}))" is entailed by General Explanatory Set Identity along with the fact that {Socrates} = {Socrates}.

Fine questions whether explanatory identity criteria should be formulated generally, using universal quantification in this way. He denies that we should try to find the grounds of individual identity and distinctness facts. Insofar as a general identity criterion entails its instances, and its instances state grounds for individual identity and distinctness facts, accepting general identity criterion may commit one to taking individual identity and distinctness facts to be grounded.

Yet, according to Fine, individual identity facts like {Socrates} = {Socrates} do not stand in need of metaphysical explanation. The question of what grounds {Socrates} = {Socrates}, Fine thinks, is a "pseudo-problem – one that we cannot take seriously as answering to any real issue about the identity of sets" (Fine 2016: 12). When providing a metaphysical explanation of set-identity, we do not care about in virtue of what is it the case that {Socrates} is identical with {Socrates}. We do not care about {Socrates} or {Napoleon} or any set in particular when we provide explanatory identity criteria for sets, the thought goes.

Instead, Fine thinks that to provide explanatory identity criteria, we should employ *generic* identity criteria: identity criteria that tell us when two *arbitrary* entities are identical or distinct. General identity criteria tell us that for any objects (or any objects of a certain kind, such as persons or sets), they are identical when some condition holds. Generic identity criteria tell us that for any arbitrary objects (or arbitrary objects of a certain kind, such as arbitrary sets or arbitrary persons), they are identical when some condition holds.

We speak of arbitrary objects of various kinds: the arbitrary integer, the arbitrary American, the arbitrary set, and so on. Arbitrary objects "represent" individual objects without themselves being individual objects. While an arbitrary object is difficult to characterize, we are familiar with the notion from various contexts. We utilize the notion of arbitrariness in our high-school and college mathematics and logic courses. Raven (2020) frames the idea as follows: "To illustrate, consider how one might explain the rule of universal generalization to students of a first formal logic course. One might say that if one can show that an *arbitrary* item a satisfies some condition f, then one may deduce that every item whatsoever satisfies that condition: $\forall x f(x)$."

Given that arbitrary objects are less familiar as an ontological category than individual objects, more needs to be said about their nature and about how arbitrary objects relate to individual objects. What is it for an arbitrary object to represent an individual object? What can we say about the relationship between the properties of the arbitrary objects and individual objects? For instance, which properties does the arbitrary American share with Dwayne The Rock Johnson (an individual American)? Unfortunately, this is not the space to explore the answers to these questions, but these and related issues are discussed by Fine (1983, 1985a, 1985b) and Horsten (2019).

Setting aside these questions about the nature of arbitrary objects, let us turn to how to use arbitrary objects in formulating identity criteria. We can modify the general identity criteria as follows:

Generic Material Leibniz's Law: For arbitrary objects x and y, $x = y \equiv (\forall P)(Px \equiv Py)$

Generic Explanatory Set-Identity: For arbitrary sets x and y, if $x = y$ then then $x = y$ is fully grounded in the fact: $(\forall z)(z \in x \equiv z \in y)$.

Fine favors formulating explanatory identity criteria for set identity generically. In Generic Explanatory Set-Identity, we should ask "in virtue of what are these two sets the same, i.e., what is it about the two arbitrary sets (considered as representative individual sets, not as objects in their own right) that would make them the same" (Fine 2016: 13)? Formulating Explanatory Set-Identity generically allows us to avoid the "pseudoproblem" of determining what explains the identity fact {Socrates} = {Socrates}.

If it is a pseudoproblem to determine what grounds individual identity and distinctness facts, then this provides a reason to formulate explanatory identity criteria generically. But it is not clear to everyone that determining the grounds of individual identity and distinctness facts is a pseudoproblem. In certain cases, we may have strong reasons to find the grounds of individual identity and distinctness facts. If I enter a teletransporter and a psychologically continuous person composed of different matter emerges from the transporter, I want to know whether that person is identical with me, and in virtue of what that person is identical or distinct from me. I do not merely care about the grounds of the identity or distinctness of arbitrary persons. I want to explain in virtue of what *that person* is identical or distinct from *me*.

Nevertheless, even if we accept that individual identity and distinctness facts are grounded, we can still formulate and accept generic identity criteria. There is room to further explore the potential advantages of generic identity criteria over general identity criteria, but I will not take a stand on which formulation to adopt in what follows.[20] The purpose of this section has been to provide an overview of types of identity criteria and the differences exhibited by them. Let us now turn our attention to one criterion of object identity in particular, Leibniz's Law.

2 The Indiscernibility of Identicals

2.1 Breaking Down Leibniz's Law

In the next three sections, I examine one proposed criterion for object identity: Leibniz's Law. Recall that Leibniz's Law states, roughly, that objects x and y are identical just in case they share all the same properties. In everyday life, we witness many confirming instances of Leibniz's Law. Distinct objects have different features. The pine tree on my block and the oak tree on my block are distinct: the pine tree produces pinecones wheareas the oak tree does not. Napoleon is distinct from Genghis Khan: Napoleon lived in France whereas Genghis Khan did not. Jane Eyre is distinct from Huckleberry Finn: Jane Eyre is an English governess whereas Huckleberry Finn is an American boy rafting down the Mississippi River.[21] And every object seems to have the same features as itself.

In the past century, the discussion of Leibniz's Law has split to focus on the two principles that comprise Leibniz's Law.[22] Contemporary philosophers decompose Leibniz's Law into *the identity of indiscernibles* and *the indiscernibility of identicals*. The identity of indiscernibles states that if x and y share all their properties, then x is identical with y. And the indiscernibility of identicals states that if x is identical with y, then x and y share all their properties.

This section concerns the indiscernibility of identicals. I will assess the identity of indiscernibles in Section 3. We interpret the formulations of Material Leibniz's Law and Modal Leibniz's Law from Section 1 as conjunctions of the identity of indiscernibles and the indiscernibility of identicals:

Material Leibniz's Law:

Material Principle of the Identity of Indiscernibles: $\forall x \forall y (\forall P (Px \equiv Py) \supset x = y)$

and

Material Principle of the Indiscernibility of Identicals: $\forall x \forall y (x = y \supset \forall P (Px \equiv Py))$

---

[20] Fine identifies additional virtues of providing generic identity criteria over general identity criteria in Fine (2016).

[21] While I will not discuss the identity and distinctness of fictional objects specifically in this element, see Caplan and Muller (2015) for a fascinating discussion of identity and fiction.

[22] Sometimes, "Leibniz's Law" is used to denote just the indiscernibility of identicals. But in this work, it denotes the conjunction of the indiscernibility of identicals and the identity of indiscernibles.

Modal Leibniz's Law:

Modal Identity of Indiscernibles: $\Box \forall x \forall y (\forall P(Px \equiv Py) \supset x = y)$

and

Modal Principle of the Indiscernibility of Identicals: $\Box \forall x \forall y (x = y \supset \forall P (Px \equiv Py))$

Explanatory Leibniz's Law, on the other hand, is more complicated. It does not take the form of a biconditional statement; as such, it does not straightforwardly decompose into a version of the identity of indiscernibles and the indiscernibility of identicals. The formulation of Explanatory Leibniz's Law from Section 1 is actually an explanatory form of the identity of indiscernibles. But we can formulate explanatory versions of the indiscernibility of identicals as well:

Explanatory Identity of Indiscernibles (F.K.A. "Explanatory Leibniz's Law"):

$\forall x \forall y$ (If $x = y$ then $x = y$ is fully grounded in the fact $\forall P(Px \equiv Py)$)

and

$\forall x \forall y$ (If $x \neq y$ then $x \neq y$ is fully grounded in the fact $\exists P((Px \lor Py)\& \sim (Px \& Py))$).

Explanatory Indiscernibility of Identicals:

$\forall x \forall y$ (If $x = y$ then $x = y$ fully grounds the fact $\forall P(Px \equiv Py)$)

and

$\forall x \forall y$ (If $x \neq y$ then $x \neq y$ fully grounds the fact $\exists P(Px \lor Py)\& \sim (Px \& Py))$)

While the Material and Modal formulations of the indiscernibility of identicals are familiar, no one, to my knowledge, has proposed or defended the Explanatory Indiscernibility of Identicals. Explanatory versions of the identity of indiscernibles (what so far has been called "Explanatory Leibniz's Law"), on the other hand, have been discussed.[23] We cannot accept both an explanatory version of the identity of indiscernibles *and* an explanatory version of the indiscernibility of identicals because ground and explanation are typically taken to be asymmetric: If P explains Q then Q does not explain P. Given that the Explanatory Identity of Indiscernibles maintains that facts of the form $\forall P(Px \equiv Py)$ explain facts of the form $x = y$, and the Explanatory Indiscernibility of Identicals takes facts of the form $\forall P(Px \equiv Py)$ to be explained by facts of the form $x = y$, we cannot accept explanatory versions of both principles.

It makes sense that we cannot accept explanatory versions of both principles, but why should we opt for an explanatory version of the identity of indiscernibles rather than an explanatory version of the indiscernibility of identicals? This has not been discussed; nevertheless, we can take a guess at the reason. Some philosophers

---

[23] See Della Rocca (2005), Burgess (2012), Shumener (2020a), and Wörner (2021).

seek to answer the question, "In virtue of what do identity and distinctness facts obtain?" (see Burgess [2012] and Shumener [2020a]). Because an explanatory version of the identity of indiscernibles maintains that identity facts hold in virtue of facts of the form $\forall P(Px \equiv Py)$, it provides an answer to this question. On the other hand, since explanatory versions of the indiscernibility of identicals tell us that facts of the form $\forall P(Px \equiv Py)$ are themselves explained by identity facts, they are not equipped to answer that question.

As remarked in Section 1, not everyone seeks to ground or explain identity and distinctness facts. So, it is possible that one could reject the Explanatory Identity of Indiscernibles and embrace the Explanatory Indiscernibility of Identicals instead. It would be interesting to explore the potential motivations for the Explanatory Indiscernibility of Identicals, but I will set aside the explanatory and modal versions of the indiscernibility of identicals in what follows.

The indiscernibility of identicals is the less controversial half of Leibniz's Law. Nevertheless, it is not without its challenges. As with the identity of indiscernibles, there are questions about how to understand the scope of the indiscernibility of identicals. Should the principle be restricted to objects – entities as cats, tables, souls, numbers, and so on? Or rather, are there versions of the indiscernibility of identicals that apply to properties as well? In other words, should we also accept that if properties F and G are identical, then F and G share all their features?[24] In what follows, I will just consider versions of the principle whose scope is limited to objects. I will also assume that properties exist and limit our focus to versions of the indiscernibility of identicals that invoke monadic properties and utilize the material conditional as well as the material biconditional.[25]

To simplify the discussion, I focus on the Material Indiscernibility of Identicals. The material version states that if x is identical with y, then x and y share all of their properties. The truth of this principle seems straightforward. Of course, if x and y are *one and the same object*, then they must share all their properties. Philosophers have proposed versions of the indiscernibility of identicals for centuries. Baxter (2018) quotes William of Ockham as follows: "But among creatures the same thing cannot be truly affirmed and truly denied of the same thing." (Baxter 2018: 1) M. M. Adams (1976) provides a helpful discussion of ways in which Ockham deploys the principle. And while much of our discussion will focus on Leibniz's adherence to the identity of indiscernibles, the indiscernibility of identicals is often associated with Leibniz as well.[26]

---

[24] See Baxter (2018) for an interesting discussion of restrictions of the indiscernibility of identicals. See Rodriguez-Pereyra (2017) for discussion of indiscernible universals.

[25] For discussion of views of Leibniz's Law that are not committed to the existence of properties, see Magidor (2011), Williamson (2001), and Hawthorne (2003).

[26] However, it has been contested whether Leibniz himself ever stated a principle that is equivalent to the indiscernibility of identicals. See Feldman (1970) and Curley (1971) for a classic discussion of this issue.

Unlike the identity of indiscernibles, the indiscernibility of identicals still enjoys widespread popularity. Some even take it to be fundamental to our understanding of identity. For example, Williamson states: "[P]roperly formulated, [the indiscernibility of identicals] embodies an insight absolutely fundamental to our understanding of the logical notion of identity ... To suppose that there are exceptions to the best statement of the law is to lose one's grip on the topic" (Williamson 2001: 285).

I will now examine some arguments that invite prima facie challenges to the indiscernibility of identicals.

2.2 Controversial Arguments Featuring the Indiscernibility of Identicals

I introduced one puzzling argument invoking the indiscernibility of identicals in Section 1. I now formulate it here. Supposing that Amelia loses a single strand of hair at 12 p.m. on Tuesday, we have the following argument:

The Hair-Loss Argument

P1. If Amelia at 11:59 a.m. is identical with Amelia at 12:01 p.m., then Amelia at 11:59 a.m. has 100,000 strands of hair if and only if Amelia at 12:01 p.m. has 100,000 strands of hair.

P2. Amelia at 11:59 a.m. has 100,000 strands of hair.

P3. Amelia at 12:01 p.m. does not have 100,000 strands of hair.

C. Amelia at 11:59 a.m. is distinct from Amelia at 12:01 p.m.

P1 is an apparent instance of the Material Indiscernibility of Identicals. This argument is surprising (at least if you have not taken a philosophy course on persistence and personal identity!) because it is plausible to think that Amelia's losing a single strand of hair would not render her numerically distinct from the being she was before the loss of the strand of hair. Philosophers have attempted to preserve a natural understanding of the referent of "Amelia" and of the meaning of "survival" upon which Amelia survives the loss of the strand of hair.[27] We can now recognize that the Hair-Loss Argument is just one member in a set of bold arguments that appeal to the indiscernibility of identicals.

Magidor (2011) provides a helpful overview of arguments that appeal to the indiscernibility of identicals, and my discussion is indebted to hers. Given that

---

[27] For discussion of arguments of this style, the reader is encouraged to consult the literature on temporary intrinsics, especially Lewis (1986), Haslanger (1989), and Eddon (2010) as well as the vast literature on personal identity and temporal parts. For excellent introductions to temporal parts, see Heller (1990), Hawley (2001), and Sider (2001).

I will not discuss every argument she mentions, I encourage the reader to consult Magidor's work on the topic.[28]

One famous application of the indiscernibility of identicals occurs in Cartesian arguments for the distinctness of the mind and the body:

The Mind–Body Distinctness Argument[29]

P1. If I (a thinking thing) am identical with my body, then I can doubt that I (a thinking thing) exist if and only if I can doubt the existence of my body.

P2. I can doubt the existence of my body.

P3. I cannot doubt that I (a thinking thing) exist.

C. I am not identical with my body.

P1 is an apparent instance of the Material Indiscernibility of Identicals. Because I can doubt the existence of my body, but I cannot doubt the existence of myself (*qua* thinking thing), it follows that I (a thinking thing) must be distinct from my body. It is surprising that such a seemingly innocuous and uncontroversial principle should support the thesis that the mind is distinct from the body. This argument shows how philosophers can appeal to the indiscernibility of identicals to support a robust philosophical position.

The indiscernibility of identicals also appears in arguments concerning material constitution. Consider a statue of a horse that is made of clay, where the clay is still wet and pliable. If we take a hammer, we can destroy the statue by pummeling the clay back into a flat shape. Doing so would destroy the horse statue, but it would not destroy the clay. This suggests, via the indiscernibility of identicals, that the statue and the lump of clay are distinct. We can capture this reasoning in standard argument form as follows:

The Statue–Lump Argument[30]

P1. If the statue is identical with the lump of clay, then the statue will survive being smashed if and only if the lump of clay will survive being smashed.

---

[28] Also see Gallois (2017)

[29] Versions of this argument are attributed to Descartes (1984 [1641]) and are much discussed in introductory philosophy and philosophy of mind courses.

[30] For an overview of this debate, see Paul (2010). For arguments of this general type, see (among many others), Baker (1997), Baxter (1988), Bennett (2004), Doepke (1982), Fine (2003), Heller (1990), Johnston (1992), Koslicki (2004), Lowe (1995), Paul (2006), Shoemaker (1999), Thomson (1983), (1998), Wiggins (2001), and Yablo (1987).

P2. The statue will not survive being smashed.

P3. The lump of clay will survive being smashed.

C. The statue and the lump of clay are distinct.

The indiscernibility of identicals supports P1 in the Statue–Lump Argument just as it supports P1 in the Mind–Body Distinctness Argument. Like the Mind–Body Distinctness Argument, the Statue–Lump Argument is controversial. If we accept the conclusion, we will maintain that there are two distinct but colocated objects, the statue and the clay. That is shocking. If someone in our art class had presented the horse-shaped lump of clay on a pedestal and had asked how many objects were located on the pedestal, most of us would have responded, "one." The conclusion of this argument demands that we respond with "at least two."

There are many arguments that belong under broadly the same family as the Mind–Body Distinctness and the Statue–Lump arguments; they purport to demonstrate the distinctness of the objects in question. I will supply two more. We can appeal to the indiscernibility of identicals to argue that certain views of personal identity are false. For instance, we can appeal to the indiscernibility of identicals in an argument against the bodily view of personhood, the view that we are identical with our bodies. Imagine that we have a teletransporter that destroys all our bodily parts and then constructs a duplicate of us from new material in another location. The duplicate remembers (or seems to remember) all our experiences up until the point of entering the teletransporter, but it is made of entirely new material. The person's original body is destroyed. Those with the intuition that the person nevertheless survives the teletransportation journey can argue that persons are distinct from their bodies.

The Person–Body Argument[31]

P1. If a person is identical with their body, then a person will survive teletransportation if and only if their body will survive teletransportation.

P2. The person will survive teletransportation.

P3. Their body will not survive teletransportation.

C. The person is not identical with their body.

---

[31] The personal identity literature contains many arguments that feature cases of this type. A historically important variant of this case is one that includes "body switches" where one person supposedly wakes up in a new body but is psychologically continuous with the person in their old body. For discussion of these cases, see Locke (1979), Williams (1970), Parfit (1971), Whiting (1999), Shoemaker (1999), and many others.

P1 is supported by the indiscernibility of identicals. Many psychological continuity theorists of personal identity and persistence may find the Person–Body Argument compelling because they maintain that for a person to survive, the person at a later time must be psychologically continuous with a person at an earlier time. If the survivor of teletransportation is psychologically continuous with the person who entered the device, that is sufficient for the person who entered the device to survive as the person who emerged from the device. Proponents of the bodily view of personal identity must find ways to undermine this argument.

Finally, these arguments are similar to ones in discussions of the thesis of composition as identity. Composition as Identity states that what it is for some individuals, the xx's, to compose an object y is for the xx's to be identical with y. The composition relation just is the identity relation. This view maintains that a table is identical with its parts. One popular objection to Composition as Identity is that it violates the indiscernibility of identicals. Here is one version of the argument against Composition as Identity. Consider a deck with fifty-two cards. We can deploy the indiscernibility in the argument as follows.

The Composition as Identity Argument[32]

P1. If the deck is identical with the fifty-two cards, then the deck is fifty-two in number if and only if the cards are fifty-two in number.

P2. The deck is not fifty-two in number.

P3. The cards are fifty-two in number.

C. The deck is not identical with the fifty-two cards in its stack.

P2 is supported because we think that the deck is *one* in number. There is only a single deck. But the cards are fifty-two in number; there are fifty-two cards. So, the deck cannot be identical with the fifty-two cards. The Composition as Identity thesis is false. This is not the only argument against the thesis of composition as identity that deploys the indiscernibility of identicals (for example, see McDaniel [2008] for a discussion of another argument).

There are at least two varieties of responses to arguments of this style. The first is to reject the indiscernibility of identicals (at least the versions of the principle formulated in Section 2.1). The second involves claiming that the indiscernibility of identicals has not been violated. I will investigate the first

---

[32] For discussion of arguments concerning composition as identity, see as a sample: Baxter (1988), van Inwagen (1994) Wallace (2011a, 2011b), McDaniel (2008) Cotnoir (2013), Cotnoir and Baxter (2014), Garland (2020), Bricker (2021), among others.

response and explore ways in which we can try to modify or reject the indiscernibility of identicals. I will also examine versions of the second response.

2.3 Rejecting the Indiscernibility of Identicals

Can we reject the indiscernibility of identicals outright? One potential way to do so is by embracing a theory of Relative Identity. While we typically think that "=" picks out the identity relation, some philosophers deny that there is a single identity relation denoted by "=" or "is identical with." This view was popularized by Geach.[33] Geach maintains that instead of a single "absolute" identity relation, we should believe in a set of relativized identity relations. He believes that there are many relations picked out by predicates of the form "is the same F as" where F is a sortal term. We may have a *same statue as* relation, a *same lump as* relation, a *same person as* relation, and a *same table as* relation. These are all identity relations, but the relative identity theorist denies the existence of a single, absolute identity relation.

Relative Identity theorists believe that objects can be identical with respect to one sortal and distinct with respect to another sortal. For instance, in the case of a statue "Statue" and a lump of clay "Lumpy," Statue may be the same lump of clay as Lumpy even though Statue is not the same statue as Lumpy. Relative Identity theorists can offer a solution to puzzles of material constitution. We can accommodate the intuition that the lump of clay and the statue are the same in one sense and distinct in another sense. They are the same in the sense of being the same lump of clay, but they are distinct in that they are not the same statue.

One prominent objection accuses the Relative Identity theory of causing trouble for set theory. We take set A to be the same set as set B if and only if A and B have the same members. But suppose that set A has x as a member and set B has y as a member. To determine whether Set A = Set B, we must determine whether x = y. Presumably "member" does not pick out a kind or sortal in the way that "lump" and "statue" do; to determine whether x and y are the same member of a set, we need a notion of absolute identity. Since it is crucial to set theory that we can determine whether two sets are the same or not, absolute identity is crucial to set theory, so the objection goes (Hawthorne 2003).[34] For our purposes, we will not delve into the arguments for and against Relative Identity. Instead, we want to know the consequences of embracing Relative Identity for the indiscernibility of identicals.

---

[33] See, for example, Geach (1967) and Geach (1973).

[34] For classic objections to relative identity, see Wiggins (1967), etc. For an overview of objections to relative identity theses, see Deutsch and Garbacz (2008).

What impact does Relative Identity have on the indiscernibility of identicals? Let us reexamine the Statue-Lump argument in light of the Relative Identity theorist's claims. The Relative Identity theorist will reject P1 of the argument. In Magidor's words, "[I]t is obvious that the proponent of relative identity would reject [the indiscernibility of identicals], if the law is interpreted as involving the notion of absolute identity: the antecedent of the law ('a is identical to b') is, according to the relative identity view, unintelligible" (Magidor 2011: 183).

Will the Relative Identity theorist accept a modified version of the indiscernibility of identicals? Perhaps, but it's not clear which version(s) can escape puzzling consequences. Suppose the Relative Identity theorist adopts a modification of the indiscernibility of identicals as follows:

Relativized Indiscernibility of Identicals: $\forall x \forall y \forall K (x$ is the same K as $y \supset \forall P$ (x has $P \equiv y$ has P))

In this statement of the indiscernibility of identicals, the x- and y-quantifiers range over objects, the P-quantifier ranges over properties, and the K-quantifier ranges over kinds or sortals. This version of the principle states that if x and y belong to the same sortal, then x and y share all their properties. Following Magidor, we can use this version of the principle to generate a variant of the Statue–Lump Argument. Suppose that "Statue" is the name of the statue and "Lumpy" is the name of the lump of clay.

Relative Statue–Lump Argument

P1. If Lumpy is the same lump of clay as Statue, then Statue is the same statue as Statue if and only if Lumpy is the same statue as Statue.

P2. Statue is the same statue as Statue.

P3. Lumpy is not the same statue as Statue.

C. Lumpy is not the same lump of clay as Statue.

P1 is an instance of the relativized indiscernibility of identicals. P2 is supposed to be trivial: Statue is the same statue as itself. P3 articulates one of the Relative Identity theorist's commitments: Lumpy is not the same statue as Statue. The conclusion is problematic because the Relative Identity theorist claims that Statue and Lumpy are the same lump of clay even though they are not the same statue. Thus, Magidor avers that the Relative Identity theorist should reject this relativized version of the indiscernibility of identicals. We have now seen how a Relative Identity theorist can reject the material version of the indiscernibility of identicals and why they may want to reject the relativized version. It is an interesting project to determine whether there is some version of the indiscernibility of identicals that the Relative Identity theorist could happily accept.

2.4 Do the Arguments Exhibit True Violations of the Indiscernibility of Identicals?

Rejecting the indiscernibility of identicals is rather uncommon. There are other approaches we can take to resist the conclusions of (at least some of) the controversial arguments mentioned in Section 2.2. I will mention two varieties of the second response following Fine's (2003) discussion. Fine considers arguments of the form:

$$\frac{\varphi(\text{x}), \sim\varphi(\text{y})}{\sim\text{x} = \text{y}}$$

This argument schema is like the ones in Section 2.2. We highlight two (supposed) properties with respect to which x and y differ, and we conclude from the fact that one has φ and the other lacks φ that x is distinct from y. Following Fine, we will examine two strategies to block arguments of this style: The referential-shift strategy and the predicational-shift strategy.

2.4.1 The Referential-Shift Strategy

Returning to the Statue–Lump Argument, suppose we reject the conclusion and affirm that the statue is identical with the lump of clay; we deny the existence of multiple, spatiotemporally coinciding entities. One way to do so is to maintain that the referent of "statue" is not the same in P1 as it is in P2. There is a *shift* in the referent of the term "statue." Perhaps "statue" refers to a physical object on some occasions and to a work of art (Magidor 2011) on others; moreover, the physical statue is identical with the lump of clay even though the work of art is not.

On this proposal, while "statue" refers to physical statues in certain contexts (including in P1), it does not do so in P2. The artwork will not survive being smashed, but the physical object will. If that's the case, then even if we accept the truth of P2, "The statue will not survive being smashed," that does not imply that we attribute the property *will not survive being smashed* to the physical statue. Thus, the proponent of the referential-shift strategy can claim that we have not established that the physical statue is distinct from the lump of clay. For this approach to be viable, we must understand what is it for "statue" to refer to a work of art in this context. Is the artwork an abstract object? If so and abstract objects lack spatiotemporal locations, then we can avoid a commitment to spatiotemporally coinciding objects. On the other hand, if the artwork still has a location, then it still shares the same location as the lump of clay. In that case, it is not clear that this approach will help us reject coincident entities. Fine discusses criticisms of the referential-shift strategy (Fine 2003: 209–12).

2.4.2 The Predicational-Shift Strategy

Another way to uphold the identity of the objects in question is to assert the existence of a *predicational shift*. Just as the referential-shift strategy states that the referent of "statue" can shift, the predicational-shift strategy states that which properties we attribute to the objects shifts. For example, when we say that the statue will not survive being smashed, we mean that the statue does not have the property *will survive as a statue* in the case where it is smashed. The predicate "will not survive" picks out the property *will not survive as a statue*. But when we say that the lump of clay will survive the smashing, we are ascribing to the clay the property *will survive as a lump of clay*. Here, the predicate "will survive" picks out the property *will survive as a lump of clay*. Once we realize that "will survive" picks out *will survive as a statue* in one context and *will survive as a lump of clay* in another context, then it is not the case that there is a property that the statue has and the clay lacks. Thus, we can accept P1–P3 of the argument but reject the conclusion. Because there is a predicational shift exhibited between P2 and P3, this is not a true violation of the indiscernibility of identicals. The proponent of the predicational-shift strategy can uphold the indiscernibility of identicals; nonetheless, questions and concerns arise for the predicational-shift strategy. For one, it's unclear exactly how the predicational shift is supposed to work. What determines, for example, when "will survive" will pick out the property *will survive as a material object*, as opposed to the property, *will survive as a lump of clay, will survive as a statue,* or *will survive as a horse statue*? There are multiple candidates onto which the predicate may shift. See Fine (2003: 212–18) for discussion of the predicational-shift strategy.

2.5 Recent Work in the Indiscernibility of Identicals

The arguments in Section 2.2 have consequences for various debates in metaphysics, such as debates over the mind–body problem, material constitution, composition, and personal identity. But similar arguments have been advanced in debates in the philosophy of language and logic. Philosophers have recently explored the appropriate logical theories for rejecting the indiscernibility of identicals. I explore the motivations of these philosophers in this section.

Frege notoriously raised examples concerning Hesperus and Phosphorous. "Hesperus" and "Phosphorous" are two names for the planet Venus. Ancient astronomers allegedly did not realize that both names picked out a single planet.

They did not know that only a single celestial body appeared in that location in the morning and in the evening. Those ancient astronomers believed "Hesperus" referred to the star that appeared in the evening ("the evening star"), and they believed "Phosphorous" referred to the star that appeared in the morning ("the morning star"). We can advance the following argument with the same structure as those earlier:

The Hesperus–Phosphorous Argument

P1. If Hesperus is identical with Phosphorous, then Hesperus is believed to rise in the morning if and only if Phosphorous is believed to rise in the morning.

P2. Phosphorous is believed (by ancient astronomers) to rise in the morning.

P3. It is not the case that Hesperus is believed (by ancient astronomers) to rise in the morning.

C. Hesperus is distinct from Phosphorous.

Given that Hesperus is identical with Phosphorous, we must explain what has gone wrong in the Hesperus–Phosphorous Argument. Frege (1892) popularized cases of this form in the context of discussing the semantic content of names. There is an extensive literature in the philosophy of language addressing what is going on in the Hesperus–Phosphorous Argument. Frege himself adopted a version of the referential-shift strategy. The names "Hesperus" and "Phosphorous" refer to Venus in many ordinary sentences, such as when we say "Hesperus is bright," "Phosphorous is massive," and so on; yet, Frege argues that the referents of "Hesperus" and "Phosphorous" shift when we describe attitudes. When we say, "Hesperus is believed (by ancient astronomers) to appear in the evening" (P2), the referent of "Hesperus" is no longer Venus; instead, the referent is what we ordinarily take to be the *sense* expressed by "Hesperus." A sense, or "mode of presentation," is an abstract, immutable entity typically expressed by a definite description. A good candidate for the sense of "Hesperus" would be that which is associated with the definite description "the celestial body appearing in the evening."[35] Unlike planets, senses are not concrete entities. Similarly in P3, the referent of "Phosphorous" is no longer Venus; instead, its referent is what we ordinarily take to be the sense expressed by the definite description "the celestial body appearing in the morning."

The phenomenon – wherein we take "Hesperus" and "Phosphorous" to co-refer to the same object even though Phosphorous is believed to shine in the

---

[35] It is unclear what exactly Frege takes the relationship is between definite descriptions and senses to be. For difficulties with Frege's notion of a sense, see Schiffer (1990).

morning and Hesperus is believed to shine in the evening – is often called "Frege's Puzzle."[36] While Frege believes that attitude reports induce referential shifts, his response to The Hesperus–Phosphorous Argument is not the only the option open to philosophers. Philosophers have defended a variety of proposals to solve the puzzle. A second way to respond to these cases is to claim that "believes" is context sensitive, and that a sentence like "Phosphorous is believed to shine in the morning while Hesperus is believed to shine in the evening" exhibits equivocation: there is a context shift midway through the sentence that leads us to resolve the context sensitivity of the first and second instances of "believes" differently.[37] A third response is to deny the inference from "x believes Hesperus is bright" to "Hesperus is such that x believes *it* is bright." If we deny this inference, then we can deny that there is one object such that x believes *it* appears in the morning and *it* does not appear in the evening.[38] These are just three of many proposed solutions to Frege's Puzzle.[39]

Predicates invoking attitudes, such as "believes," "desires," "doubts," and so on, are often called "opaque" following Quine (1960). A predicate is opaque when applying that predicate to (intuitively) coreferential terms does not always yield sentences with the same truth-value. But "opaque" also applies to predicates that are unrelated to attitudes. For instance, "will survive being smashed" may be opaque as well. Supposing that "Statue" and "Lumpy" are coreferential names, substituting "Lumpy" for "Statue" in the sentence, "Statue will survive being smashed," will yield a sentence with a different truth-value. While the original sentence is false, the new sentence, "Lumpy will survive being smashed," is true. We have already seen that one can deploy the referential-shift strategy when responding the Statue–Lump argument as well as to the Hesperus–Phosphorous Argument.

These cases have caught the attention of logicians and metaphysicians working on the indiscernibility of identicals. Recently, Bacon and Russell (2019), as well as Caie, Goodman, and Lederman (2020), have written about the phenomenon of opacity. Instead of arguing that opaque predicates induce referential shifts as Frege thought, Bacon and Russell explore the idea that the behavior of opaque predicates indicates a genuine problem for the indiscernibility of identicals. They explore rejecting specific instances of the indiscernibility of identicals. This is a logic-oriented approach to the puzzle because, unlike some philosophers of language working on the topic, Bacon and Russell are not primarily interested in the semantics of names – nor are they focused on

---

[36] Although, the term "Frege's Puzzle" is also used to refer to the related problem of why the claim "Hesperus = Phosphorous" and "Hesperus = Hesperus" differ in their cognitive significance.

[37] See Dorr (2014) for discussion of context shifts.

[38] See Kripke (2005) and Salmon (2010) for discussion.

[39] For an overview of Frege's puzzle and responses, see Nelson (2019).

metaphysical debates concerning relative versus absolute relations of identity. Rather, they strive to understand and develop the appropriate logic for rejecting the indiscernibility of identicals.

Bacon and Russell discuss different routes to rejecting the indiscernibility of identicals. They call attention to three claims. (Note that their formulations differ slightly from the formulations of the indiscernibility of identicals and its instances set out in this Element because Bacon and Russell's formulations do not involve a material biconditional in the consequent.)

$$L(xyX){:}\forall x\forall y\forall X(x = y \rightarrow Xx \rightarrow Xy)$$

$$L(xy){:}\forall x\forall y(x = y \rightarrow Bx \rightarrow By)$$

$$L()\text{: } a = b \rightarrow Ba \rightarrow Bb \ ^{40}$$

The first claim, $L(xyX)$, is a higher-order generalization that intuitively says that for *any* objects x, y, and predicate X, if x is identical with y then x has X only if y has X. The second is a first-order generalization that says for any x and y, and for some specific predicate B, if $x = y$, then x has B only if y has B. The third claim says that for some specific objects a and b, and some specific predicate B, if $a = b$, then a has B only if b has B. This is going too quickly: to fully grasp their project, we need to investigate how they are thinking about their formal framework and higher-order quantification. Bacon and Russell deploy a theory of types, but, for our purposes, the intuitive understanding of these claims will do.

Bacon and Russell describe three ways of attacking the indiscernibility of identicals. The first is to deny the truth of $L(xyX)$. This is naturally the approach we would take were we to reject the indiscernibility of identicals: to reject the indiscernibility of identicals is just to take the principle itself to be false.[41] But Bacon and Russell express misgivings with this approach and consider two other approaches. The first is to accept $L(xyX)$ and reject the inference from $L(xy)$ to $L()$. The second is to accept $L(xyX)$ and reject the inference from $L(xyX)$ to $L(xy)$. Both latter approaches involve what Bacon and Russell call "failures of exportability." From the perspective of those interested in logic and metaphysics, these present interesting alternatives to rejecting the statement of the indiscernibility of identicals in $L(xyX)$. Perhaps we can retain the plausibility of the indiscernibility of identicals by upholding $L(xyX)$ while still avoiding troubling cases by rejecting certain inference principles. Determining which method of attacking the indiscernibility of identicals (if any) yields the most

---

[40] Bacon and Russell associate arrows to the right.
[41] For further exploration of these approaches, see Caie, Goodman, and Lederman (2020).

satisfying logical system is a fruitful and exciting enterprise. This is an emerging area of research that invokes overlapping debates in logic, metaphysics, and philosophy of language.

3 The Identity of Indiscernibles

This section concerns the more controversial half of Leibniz's Law, the identity of indiscernibles. I will discuss some historical and contemporary formulations of this principle.

3.1 Leibniz and the Identity of Indiscernibles

3.1.1 Formulating the Identity of Indiscernibles

According to the identity of indiscernibles, for individuals x and y to differ in number, they must differ in some respect or other. Although the principle was popularized by Leibniz, it appears in philosophical works predating Leibniz. For one, the principle is also attributed to the Stoics.[42] And Leibniz himself believed Thomas Aquinas held a restricted version of this principle. Leibniz (1696) states: "Thomas Aquinas has already remarked that two angels cannot be perfectly similar, and the same reason holds concerning souls" (Leibniz, Letter to Burnett of 17 March 1696; G III 176–7).

Leibniz takes the principle to apply to individuals more generally:[43]

> I have also remarked that . . . no two individual things can be perfectly similar, and that they must always differ more than numerically. (Leibniz (1704): A 6 6 57/cf. NE 57)

> The principle of individuation reduces, in individuals, to the principle of distinction of which I have just been speaking. If two individuals were perfectly similar and equal and (in a word) indistinguishable by themselves, there would be no principle of individuation . . . I remember a great princess, of outstanding intelligence, saying one day while wandering around her garden that she did not believe there were two perfectly similar leaves. An ingenious gentleman who was walking with her believed that it would be easy to find some: but although he searched for them a great deal, he became convinced by his own eyes that a difference could always be observed[44] (Leibniz (1704) A 6 6 230–1/cf. NE 230–1)

---

[42] See E. Lewis (1995) for discussion of the Stoic commitment to the identity of indiscernibles.

[43] See Rodriguez-Pereyra (2014) for a more detailed list of Leibniz excerpts and for an in-depth treatment of the issues and questions discussed.

[44] These Leibniz passages can be found in Rodriguez-Pereyra (2014: 17–18).

In the above passages, Leibniz remarks that no distinct individuals can be "perfectly similar," but it is controversial whether Leibniz would accept the material, modal, or explanatory formulations of the identity of indiscernibles.[45]

There is also a question of exactly how wide a scope the identity of indiscernibles is supposed to take for Leibniz: does it apply to abstract objects in addition to concrete ones? Rodriguez-Pereyra (2014: 20) argues that Leibniz intends the principle to have maximal scope: " [I]t says that things – whatever kind of things they are – are not perfectly similar, or, in a stronger formulation, that there cannot be perfectly similar things, whatever kind of things they are."

3.1.2 A Restriction to Internal Differences

At certain points, Leibniz apparently claims that for individuals to differ numerically, they must differ in their *intrinsic* properties. Intrinsic properties are those that an individual has solely in virtue of how it is in itself or solely in virtue of its parts. For instance, properties such as *having a heart* and *being circular*[46] may count as intrinsic, while *standing next to McDonald's* and *carrying an octopus* are presumably extrinsic properties. An object does not instantiate those latter properties solely in virtue of how it is in itself: whether the individual instantiates them also depends on the location of the McDonald's and the cooperation of the octopus in question.

In multiple locations, Leibniz states that distinct individuals must differ "internally":

> [T]here cannot be two things that differ from each other only in respect of place and time, but it is always necessary that there be some other internal difference. (Leibniz 1973 [1696]: 133)

> There must always be, besides the difference of time and of place, an internal principle of distinction, even if there are many things of the same species; it is nevertheless true that none of them are ever perfectly similar. (Leibniz 1996 [1704]: NE 230)[47]

Rodriguez-Pereyra (2014: 3) understands Leibniz's appeals to internality in terms of intrinsicality. Versions of the identity of indiscernibles that are restricted to intrinsic properties will state that if objects x and y share all and only the same intrinsic properties, then x is identical with y. No distinct objects are wholly intrinsically alike. This seems to imply that there cannot be perfect or exact duplicates of objects in the universe.

---

[45] See Hacking (1975), Jauernig (2008), and Rodriquez-Pereyra (2014) for discussion of the modal force of Leibniz's identity of indiscernibles. For the suggestion that Leibniz upheld an explanatory version of the principle, see Della Rocca (2005).

[46] However, see Skow (2007) for someone who argues that shape properties are extrinsic.

[47] These Leibniz passages can also be found in Rodriguez-Pereyra (2014: 17–18).

The restriction to intrinsic properties makes it easier (in principle) to find counterexamples to the identity of indiscernibles. Recall that in Section 1, we remarked that even if we had two duplicate spheres in the actual world, we can still use Material Leibniz's Law to distinguish them: Actual Castor is 50 miles from Tuscaloosa while Actual Pollux is 100 miles from Tuscaloosa. The spheres differ in that Actual Castor instantiates the property *50 miles from Tuscaloosa* while Actual Pollux does not. But *50 miles from Tuscaloosa* and *100 miles from Tuscaloosa* are extrinsic properties of Actual Castor and Actual Pollux. These are not properties the spheres have solely in virtue of themselves. On the other hand, cases like that of Actual Castor and Actual Pollux may threaten Material Leibniz's Law (the Material Identity of Indiscernibles, specifically) if the principle is restricted to intrinsic properties. Actual Castor and Actual Pollux seem to share their intrinsic properties.

Let us look at a passage from Leibniz where he seems to anticipate cases resembling the Max Black spheres. In his letter to Casati, Leibniz says:

> Certainly, if A and B are diverse then without doubt they will have a diversity, or a principle of distinction, in themselves; in themselves, I emphasise it so as not to have to think of external objects. For let us suppose that all external objects are annihilated and that two material spheres (with which I shall now replace the eggs) remain alone in imaginary space, then I say that by no one, however great be his intellect, indeed neither by an angel nor even by God, can these two perfectly equal and similar spheres be distinguished. For the principle of distinction would not be in themselves (given the hypothesis of the opponents), or in external objects given the hypothesis of the removal of external objects, nor can the parts of imaginary space that surround the spheres be distinguished from each other. But it is absurd that there are two distinct things, which cannot be distinguished even by an infinite intellect. (Leibniz, quoted in Rodriguez-Pereyra 2014: 84–85)

This passage is significant for multiple reasons. First, it is another location where Leibniz articulates something like an intrinsicality condition on the principle of the identity of indiscernibles; he states, "[I]f A and B are diverse when without doubt they will have a diversity, or a principle of distinction, in themselves." Second, Leibniz anticipates the type of case that is often invoked as a counterexample to the identity of indiscernibles, but here Leibniz uses the case to support the principle. Leibniz asks us to imagine that there are individuals (spheres) that are intrinsically alike (we can suppose that they have the same mass, shape, size, temperature, and so on), but are yet distinct. Then, Leibniz supposes, we could imagine those spheres in an otherwise empty universe. If so, then we would have no way to distinguish the spheres, either by their intrinsic properties or by their extrinsic properties. But if the spheres cannot be distinguished either by their intrinsic or extrinsic properties, then not even an "infinite intellect" can distinguish the spheres. But Leibniz believes "[I]t is absurd that there are two distinct things, which cannot be distinguished even by an infinite intellect." Thus, we should conclude that individuals must differ in their intrinsic features.

Contemporary versions of the identity of indiscernibles often maintain that objects must differ with respect to their qualitative or nontrivial properties, but they do not typically maintain that objects need to differ with respect to their intrinsic properties. So, in this respect, Leibniz's version of the principle is stronger than many contemporary formulations.

3.1.3 Leibnizian Applications of the Principle

Among other applications, Leibniz deploys the principle to argue against the existence of Democritean atoms and empty space. Leibniz says:

> Hence it cannot happen in nature that two bodies are at the same time perfectly equal and similar. Also, bodies which differ in place must express their place, that is, their surroundings, and thus they are not to be distinguished so much by place or by an extrinsic denomination alone, as such things are commonly conceived. Hence bodies, in the commonly assumed way, like the atoms of the Democriteans and the perfect globules of the Cartesians, cannot exist in nature. (G II 250/cf. DV 259)

Leibniz's idea is that no two bodies can be perfectly equal and similar – given the identity of indiscernibles. Thus, we should reject the existence of atoms and "globules" that are exactly "equal and similar."

Leibniz also deploys the identity of indiscernibles to argue against the existence of regions of empty space. If a region of empty space were to exist, then each part of the region would be intrinsically identical to every other part. Thus, by the identity of indiscernibles, those parts of empty space cannot exist:

> There is no vacuum. For different parts of empty space would be perfectly similar and mutually congruent and could not be distinguished from one another, and thus they would differ only in number, which is absurd. (cited in Rodriguez-Pereyra 2014: 157)

Leibniz appeals to the identity of indiscernibles in other contexts as well. Leibniz invokes the principle in his discussion of whether the soul could be an "empty tablet" and in his discussion of the nature of action.[48]

---

[48] As a sample, see Leibniz (1996). See Rodriguez-Pereyra (2014) for discussion.

3.2 Contemporary Formulations of the Identity of Indiscernibles

Let us turn to contemporary discussion of the principle. While most philosophers in the twentieth and twenty-first centuries do not have the same objectives as Leibniz in promoting the identity of indiscernibles, they continue to be interested in the identity of indiscernibles as a principle of object individuation, as potentially providing a test – and perhaps even an explanation – of the numerical identity and distinctness of individuals.

For the most part, contemporary discussion of the identity of indiscernibles has not focused on providing arguments for accepting the identity of indiscernibles. But there are notable exceptions. For instance, Della Rocca (2005) argues for the identity of indiscernibles. Della Rocca believes that the identity of indiscernibles allows us to rule out the existence of multiple, colocated individuals. If we are sitting at a desk, it is natural to believe that there is one desk in front of us. But how can we be sure that there are not 10, 100, or 1,000 colocated, indiscernible desks in front of us? If the principle of the identity of indiscernibles is false, then it is not clear that we can rule out this possibility. One response to this argument, as advocated by Hawley (2009), is that we may have other ways to rule out the existence of such colocated, indiscernible objects. Hawley suggests that we can appeal to principles of ontological parsimony to rule out the existence of multiple, colocated tables, at least in the actual world. Hawley states, "[O]rdinary methodological principles direct us towards quantitative parsimony: other things being equal, posit as few objects as are necessary to explain the phenomena" (104).[49]

Contemporary discussion of the identity of indiscernibles has focused on two related issues: (1) formulating a nontrivial version of the principle and (2) responding to purported counterexamples to the identity of indiscernibles. In the remainder of this section, we will discuss (1). In section 4, we will discuss (2).

While Leibniz states that individuals must exhibit an internal difference to differ numerically, contemporary formulations of the principle do not have an internality or intrinsicality condition. Without a restriction to intrinsic features, we can use the principle to distinguish individuals on the basis, say, of their spatial relations to other objects. For instance, one characteristic that distinguishes Germany from China is that Germany shares a border with France while

---

[49] Goodman (ms.) also offers an intriguing line of support for the identity of indiscernibles based on the acceptance of the principle of conditional excluded middle. The principle of conditional excluded middle states that "either if it were the case that ϕ, it would be the case that ψ, or, if it were the case that ϕ, it would be the case that not-ψ." (Goodman [ms.]: 1). Although conditional excluded middle is controversial, Goodman shows that the principle entails the identity of indiscernibles.

China does not. But *sharing a border with France* is not an intrinsic property. Whether an object has that property depends in part on the nature of an individual (France) distinct from it. Contemporary formulations of the identity of indiscernibles typically allow at least some extrinsic properties to serve as distinguishing properties of individuals.

After dropping the restriction to intrinsic properties, we may try to uphold at least one of our original, unrestricted characterizations of the identity of indiscernibles. Let us look at the material version.

Material Identity of Indiscernibles: $\forall x \forall y (\forall P(Px \equiv Py) \supset x = y)$

One problem is that, without any restriction, the identity of indiscernibles is in danger of being trivial. The triviality arises if both (a) the P-quantifier ranges over all properties, and (b) we have an abundant conception of properties. An abundantist conception of properties admits not only "sparse" properties – those corresponding to fundamental or "natural" properties – into our ontology, but it also admits a wide variety of properties that do not count as fundamental or natural. Fundamental properties include those from our best scientific theories, such as determinate quantitative properties like *5 kg mass* and $-1.602 \times 10^{\wedge} - 19$ *electric charge*. In addition to such properties, an abundantist would typically admit the existence of properties like, *five meters from McDonald's*, *identical with Barack Obama*, *being either a horse or a leprechaun*, and so on.

If we accept an unrestricted version of the identity of indiscernibles, then we can easily distinguish objects on the basis of the properties in the abundantist's arsenal. We may use an unrestricted version of the identity of indiscernibles to distinguish France and Germany on the basis of the former having the property *being identical with France* and the latter lacking that property. We are now in danger of trivializing the principle. If this is how we can use the identity of indiscernibles to distinguish France and Germany, then the principle is "a useless tautology" in Max Black's (1952: 153) words (note that Black's paper is in a dialogue format, and "A" and "B" are Black's interlocutors):

> A[:] ... If two things, a and b, are given, the first has the property of being identical with a. Now b cannot have this property, for else b would be a, and we should have only one thing, not two as assumed. Hence a has at least one property, which b does not have, that is to say the property of being identical with a. B[:] This is a roundabout way of saying nothing, for 'a has the property of being identical with a' means no more than 'a is a.' When you begin to say 'a is ...' I am supposed to know what thing you are referring to as 'a' and I expect to be told something about that thing. But when you end the sentence with the words '... is a' I am left still waiting. The sentence 'a is a' is a useless tautology.

Rodriguez-Pereyra (2017) argues that we need to avoid triviality to have a metaphysically serious version of the principle. To distinguish individuals x and y, the identity of indiscernibles should not allow us to appeal to the properties *being x* and *being y*. To avoid triviality, we should impose a restriction on the types of properties appealed to in the identity of indiscernibles.

Why is triviality worrisome? Black seems to think that appealing to trivializing properties like *being France* or *being identical with a* is problematic because these properties are uninformative: the concern with a property like *being identical with a* is that we "expect" to be "told something about" a when we see the construction "a is ... ." But given that a's *being identical with* a just conveys the fact that a is a, we are still left "waiting" to learn something about a.

Rodriguez-Pereyra also seems to be primarily concerned with the lack of informativeness. Rodriguez-Pereyra believes that, given the controversial status and the purported counterexamples to the principle, the identity of indiscernibles should not be interpreted as a trivial thesis. We can expand on this thought: if the identity of indiscernibles is trivial, it cannot be used as a useful principle of individuation. But in formulating the principle, we were searching for a useful principle of individuation – a principle that allows us to distinguish individuals that will help us in our other metaphysical pursuits. Thus, we should strive to formulate a nontrivial version of the principle of the identity of indiscernibles.

If we accept an explanatory version of the identity of indiscernibles, then the threat of triviality may have a different character. Invoking trivial properties may lead to a circular explanation of identity. Suppose that a has the property *is identical with a*. Note that the fact a *is identical with a* is not necessarily the same fact as a = a. The former fact, a *is identical with a*, involves an individual (a) instantiating a monadic property, *being identical with a*. On the other hand, the fact a = a involves a's standing in a binary relation (*is identical with* or =) to itself. When I italicize *is identical with a*, this indicates that we are discussing a monadic property, not the binary identity relation. If a = a is partially grounded or explained by $\forall P(Pa \equiv Pa)$, and one monadic property that a has is *being identical with a*, then a = a will be at partially explained by a *is identical with a* = a *is identical with a*. This follows from the fact that universal generalizations, such as $\forall P(Pa \equiv Pa)$, are at least partially explained by their instances. But the biconditional a *is identical with a* $\equiv$ a *is identical with a* in turn is explained by each of its obtaining sides (when the sides obtain). Thus, given transitivity, a = a will be partially explained by a's having the monadic property *being identical with a*. If the fact of a's *being identical with a* is "nothing over and above" a = a, or in some sense explanatorily presupposes a = a, then we will violate irreflexivity: a fact cannot (even partially) explain itself.

But is it true that the fact a *is identical with a* explanatorily presupposes
a = a? Although this seems intuitive, we have not conclusively established that
a *is identical with a* explanatorily presupposes a = a. That is not to say an
explanatory circularity is not present. Rather, we need to spell out exactly how
the circularity arises. Nevertheless, the spectre of this circularity may suffice to
motivate philosophers to try to restrict explanatory versions of the principle.

3.3 Avoiding Triviality

One way to avoid triviality is to restrict the principle of the identity of indiscernibles to qualitative properties. For a material version of the principle, we
would do so as follows:

Material Qualitative Identity of Indiscernibles: $\forall x \forall y (\forall P_{\text{qualitative}} (Px \equiv Py)$
$\supset x = y)$

We subscript the P-quantifier with "qualitative," signifying that the thesis is
restricted to qualitative properties. For any x and y, if x and y share all their
qualitative properties, then they are identical. We can place similar restrictions
on the modal and explanatory versions of the principles.

It is difficult to fully define "qualitative properties," but we know which
properties should be considered as quintessentially nonqualitative: properties
like *being France* or *being identical with Obama* should not count as qualitative
properties. Intuitively, nonqualitative properties involve or require the existence of
particular individuals. They include properties such as *being identical with
Obama, being the father of Obama, being identical with a,* and *being 10 meters
from the Eiffel Tower.* The triviality concern for the identity of indiscernibles arises
from the presence of nonqualitative properties. If we attempt to distinguish a and
b by claiming a has the property *identical with a* and b has the property *identical
with b*, then the fear is that the principle is rendered uninformative. Hence, we
have reason to restrict the identity of indiscernibles to qualitative properties.

There are many different accounts of the qualitative/nonqualitative
distinction.[50] We do not have the space to investigate every account here, but
I will briefly mention two approaches to characterizing the distinction.

---

[50] A series of interesting articles on the qualitative/nonqualitative distinction have been published
over the past two decades. Carmichael (2016) and Hawley (2009) advocate for a notion of
nonqualitativeness that treats properties like *being identical with redness* (in Carmichael's
[2016: 311] case) and *composing something* (in Hawley's [2009: 469] case) as nonqualitative
even though they do not involve individuals in the same way as *being identical with Obama* or
standing next to Merkel do. Plate (in press) develops a view of qualitativeness descendent from
Carnap. Hoffman-Kolss (2019) argues for a hyperintensional account of qualitativeness. And
Cowling (2015) argues that we should treat the qualitative/nonqualitative distinction as
primitive.

R. M. Adams (1979: 6) provides an influential characterization of qualitativeness. Adams calls qualitative properties "suchnesses" and nonqualitative properties "thisnesses." According to Adams, a thisness "is the property of being identical with a certain particular individual … my property of being identical with me, your property of being identical with you, etc." Adams offers a recursive definition of a qualitative property, or "suchness," by first defining a basic suchness and then maintaining that a suchness is either a basic suchness or "constructed out of" basic suchnesses.

Here are the three criteria that Adams (1979: 7–9) believes a basic suchness must meet: (1) It must not be a thisness or equivalent to a thisness. (2) It cannot be a property of being related to a particular individual or to that individual's thisness. And (3) a basic suchness "is not a property of being identical with or related in one way or another to an extensionally defined set that has an individual among its members, or among its members' members, or among its members' members' members, etc." For example, if *being a college student* were defined as the property of *being a member of the set* {*a, b, c, d,* …} where a, b, c, and d are college students, then *being a college student* would not be a basic suchness on Adams' account.[51] With this characterization of a basic suchness at hand, Adams offers a recursive definition of a suchness in general: A suchness is either a basic suchness or constructed out of basic suchnesses.

We can also characterize the qualitative/nonqualitative distinction by appeal to Lewisian (Lewis 1983) natural properties. Monadic natural properties are those that "carve nature at its joints."[52] Perfectly natural and relatively natural properties will intuitively not be identity-involving. Examples of natural properties include the ones found in our best physical theories, such as determinate mass and charge properties. Natural properties are supposed to be intrinsic, determinate, and responsible for objective resemblance between individuals. In addition to perfectly natural properties, there are also relatively natural properties. For example, a disjunctive property like *grue* (which is the property of *being green and observed before some future time t or blue and observed after* t) will be less natural than a color property like *green*. And a property such as *being a martini* will be less natural than properties found in our best chemical theories, such as *being H_2O*.

According to Eddon (2011: 5), this strategy characterizes "the qualitative properties as those that globally supervene on the perfectly natural properties and relations." Properties of type A globally supervene on properties of type B just in case, if two worlds have the same distribution of B-properties, then

---

[51] Although, I am not advocating this definition of *being a college student*!

[52] See Lewis (1986), Langton and Lewis (1998), Bricker (2008), and Dorr (2019) for discussion of this style of proposal.

they have the same distribution of A properties. So, properties like *being circular* will be qualitative on this account if, when we duplicate the distribution of natural properties and relations (all the properties and relations from our physical theories), we will find the same pattern of circular objects. However, Eddon raises the concern that this account of qualitativeness is in danger of treating identity-involving properties as qualitative if there do not exist two distinct possible worlds with exactly the same patterns of natural properties and relations. In that case, properties like *being identical with Obama* will trivially count as qualitative. For this and other issues, see Eddon (2011).

Restricting the identity of indiscernibles to qualitative properties is not the only way to construct a nontrivial version of the identity of indiscernibles. Rodriguez-Pereyra (2017) argues that there is a notion of a "non-trivializing" property that may include certain intuitively nonqualitative properties as nontrivial, and, nevertheless, this notion can be used to formulate a nontrivial version of the identity of indiscernibles. According to Rodriguez-Pereyra (2017), F is a trivializing property when individuals differing with respect to F only requires that they differ numerically. A property like *being identical with Obama* will be trivializing. For x and y to differ with respect to this property only requires them to differ with respect to who they are numerically identical with. But a property like *being the father of Obama* can count as a nontrivial property even though it involves a specific object (Obama). Objects differ with respect to this property when they differ with respect to their "fatherhood." To differ in this way is not to differ *merely* numerically. We can now restrict the identity of indiscernibles to nontrivializing properties in the same way we restricted it to qualitative properties. Here is the material version of the principle:

Material Nontrivial Identity of Indiscernibles: $\forall x \forall y (\forall P_{non-trivializing} (Px \equiv Py) \supset x = y)$

We have now stated two ways of restricting the identity of indiscernibles so that it is a nontrivial thesis. There are many delicate issues surrounding the proper characterization of qualitative and nontrivializing properties, but we must now turn our attention to alleged counterexamples to the identity of indiscernibles.

4 Counterexamples to the Identity of Indiscernibles and Alternatives to Leibniz's Law

In this section, I discuss alleged counterexamples to the identity of indiscernibles and responses to them. I demarcate between the family of responses that preserves the identity of indiscernibles and the family of responses that rejects the identity of indiscernibles.

4.1 The Possibility of Indiscernible yet Distinct Objects

This style of case should now be familiar from previous sections. Black asks us to imagine a universe in which the only items in existence are two spheres, "Castor" and "Pollux", that are indistinguishable on the basis of their physical characteristics. They have the same mass, color, temperature, density, circumference, and so on. Nevertheless, we are supposed to imagine there being *two* such spheres. If this is metaphysically possible, it presents a potential counterexample to the Modal Identity of Indiscernibles. The problem is that these spheres appear to be indiscernible with respect to their properties that do not involve identity. The only types of properties (at least at first glance) by which they could be distinguished seem to be identity-involving properties, such as *being identical with Castor* and *being identical with Pollux*.

As a reminder, this sparse scenario does not provide a counterexample to the Material Identity of Indiscernibles nor to the Explanatory Identity of Indiscernibles. The Material Identity of Indiscernibles only provides us with a generalized material conditional: for any individuals x and y, if x and y share all their features, then x is identical with y. The Max Black case does not present us with indiscernible yet distinct spheres residing among us. Likewise, the Explanatory Identity of Indiscernibles only tells us that if x = y, then x and y's sharing all their features explains this identity fact, and if x and y are distinct, then their differing with respect to some feature explains their distinctness. The Explanatory Identity of Indiscernibles does not tell us that, in every possible world, if x ≠ y, x ≠ y is explained by x and y's differing with respect to some property. Nevertheless, those interested in exploring explanatory versions of the identity of indiscernibles take Max Black-style counterexamples to potentially threaten explanatory versions of the principle as well.[53] This indicates that they suspect the principle should have modal force. We will return to a discussion of explanatory principles in Section 4.3.

Several responses have been proposed to the Max Black cases. One family of responses argues that the Max Black scenarios do not constitute a genuine threat to the identity of indiscernibles. We witnessed in Section 2 that Leibniz considered a similar scenario in his letter to Casati and rejected it outright. Contemporary philosophers have offered their own reasons why the Max Black scenarios do not successfully challenge the identity of indiscernibles. We will consider three such responses.

---

[53] See Burgess (2012), Shumener (2020a), and Wörner (2021).

4.2 Contemporary Approaches to Upholding the Identity of Indiscernibles

The first response claims that we are inoculated against the threat posed by Castor and Pollux once we provide the correct interpretation of the Modal Identity of Indiscernibles. If we are abundantists about properties, and the formulation of the principle does not restrict the types of properties under consideration, then the Castor and Pollux scenario is not troublesome because we can invoke identity-involving properties to distinguish Castor and Pollux. Castor has the property *being Castor* while Pollux lacks that property and instead has the property *being Pollux*.[54] This response will only succeed if (a) we countenance such properties in our ontology, and (b) we have an adequate response to the concern that allowing such properties to fall under the scope of the principle trivializes the identity of indiscernibles. In undertaking (b), the proponent of this response must either show that admitting identity-involving properties into the scope of the principle does not trivialize the principle or – if it does trivialize the principle – why we should regard the identity of indiscernibles as a trivial principle.

Can the proponent of the identity of indiscernibles respond to the Max Black cases while still restricting the principle so that it does not range over properties like *being Castor* and *being Pollux*? Perhaps we can appeal to different relational properties that Castor and Pollux have to distinguish them. For instance, Castor has the property of being *five meters from Pollux* while Pollux has the property of *being five meters from Castor*. The relational properties *being five meters from Castor* and *being five meters from Pollux* distinguish Castor and Pollux. Whether this proposal is successful depends on whether such properties are admissible under the identity of indiscernibles. These are presumably nonqualitative properties in that they involve particular objects (Castor and Pollux). So, we apparently cannot appeal to these properties in a modal formulation of the identity of indiscernibles that is restricted to qualitative properties. However, while the properties *being five meters from Castor* and *being five meters from Pollux* involve specific individuals, it is not obvious that they count as identity-involving or trivializing properties.[55] Thus, whether we can distinguish Castor and Pollux on the basis of these properties depends on which restriction of the principle we adopt.

The second response to the Max Black cases posits that there is only a single sphere that resides in multiple locations (see O'Leary-Hawthorne [1995]). O'Leary-Hawthorne advances this proposal in the context of discussing how the identity of indiscernibles relates to the bundle theory. Bundle theorists – at least the ones we consider here – believe that concrete particulars are nothing

---

[54] For more on this style of response, see Adams (1979).
[55] See Rodriguez-Pereyra (2006), Hawley (2009), and Wörner (2021) for discussion.

over and above bundles of properties or universals. For example, the bundle theorist does not think of a brown wooden table as a substance instantiating various properties; instead, the table is just a bundle of properties, including properties like *wooden, brown, having legs*, and so on. Castor and Pollux are bundles of the same qualitative properties. They are both bundles of the qualitative properties: *spherical, 5 kg mass, being composed of iron*, and so on. The bundle theorist must explain how to identify or distinguish these bundles. O'Leary-Hawthorne's proposal is that we have just a single bundle that is both colocated with itself and five meters from itself.

This proposal is surprising, but it may not be as radical as one would initially think. Bundle theorists understand properties to be universals, and they take concrete particulars to be bundles of universals. Universals are already multiply located. Philosophers positing universals believe that one and the same universal, *blueness*, is located in the sky and in the Manchester City official football uniform, for example. Given that bundle theorists already believe that universals are multiply located, and given that concrete particulars just are bundles of universals, it is not so surprising that bundles of properties can be multiply located as well. Hawley (2009) nevertheless raises some confounding questions for this proposal. If this is a multiply located bundle, does it have 5 kg mass or does it have 10 kg mass? If we were to countenance two spheres, we would typically say that each sphere is 5 kg and that the sum of their masses is 10 kg. But it is less clear what to say when there is only a single sphere bundle that is multiply located.

4.3 Rejecting the Identity of Indiscernibles: Alternative Principles of Object-Individuation

The third response is to replace the identity of indiscernibles with a different principle of object individuation. There are many proposals for doing so.[56] We will briefly examine four such proposals: the Weak Discernibility Proposal, the Parthood Proposal, the Existence Proposal, and the Zero-Grounding Proposal.[57]

---

[56] See Burgess (2012).

[57] In the discussion of alternatives to the identity of indiscernibles, I will continue to consider identity criteria that are not restricted to categories or types of entities. I will not discuss separate identity criteria for properties, for material objects, for abstract objects, and so on. Yet, some philosophers believe that we should provide separate identity criteria for entities in different ontological categories, or for entities falling under different "sortals". Identity criteria should be "sortal-relative" in Lowe's (1989) terms. Positing sortal-relative identity criteria does not require that we posit a multitude of identity *relations* (as discussed in Section 2.3). We may instead claim that all entities stand in one and the same identity relation to themselves; nevertheless, we posit separate identity criteria for entities falling under different ontological categories or sortals. For discussion of sortal-relative identity criteria, see, for instance, Lowe, (1989), Linnebo (2005), Klev (2017), and Mooney (in press). The reader is also encouraged to consult Thomasson's (2014) discussion of "co-application conditions" in *Ontology Made Easy*.

4.3.1 The Weak Discernibility Proposal

The versions of the identity of indiscernibles we have examined aim to distinguish objects on the basis of their monadic properties. The Weak Discernibility Proposal distinguishes objects not on the basis of their monadic properties, but instead by the polyadic relations they stand in to each other. Following Quine (1976), objects x and y are *weakly discernible* as long they stand in irreflexive relations to each other. An irreflexive relation is one that no object stands in to itself. That is, if binary relation R is irreflexive, then ~Rxx. Objects can be weakly discernible even if they have the same mass, shape, color, temperature, and other intuitively qualitative properties. Castor and Pollux are weakly discernible because they stand in the *five meters from* relation to each other, and the *five meters from* relation is irreflexive.[58] Thus, if we distinguish objects on the basis of weak discernibility, we can distinguish the Max Black spheres. Here is a material version of the Weak Discernibility Proposal:

Material Weak Discernibility: $\forall x \forall y (x = y \equiv x$ and y are weakly indiscernible)

We can construct a modal version by introducing a necessity operator in front of the universal generalization. Shumener (2020a) also considers an explanatory version of the Weak Discernibility Proposal.[59] I will not distinguish between these versions of Weak Discernibility. While the Weak Discernibility Proposal apparently can distinguish between Castor and Pollux without invoking identity-involving properties, not everyone is willing to appeal to weak discernibility in this context. One concern raised by French (2006) and Hawley (2006, 2009) is that the appeal to irreflexive relations is inappropriate in a principle of object individuation. French states the point as follows:

> There is the worry that the appeal to irreflexive relations in order to ground the individuality of the objects which bear such relations involves a circularity: in order to appeal to such relations, one has to already individuate the particles which are so related and the numerical diversity of the particles has been presupposed by the relation which hence cannot account for it. (French and Krause 2006: 5)

---

[58] However, the irreflexivity of the *five meters from* relation would be contested by those who subscribe to O'Leary Hawthorne's response above.

[59] Shumener's (2020b) explanatory version of the Weak Discernibility Proposal is as follows:

Explanatory Weak discernibility:
When x = y, the fact that x is identical with y is fully grounded in the fact that x and y only stand in reflexive relations to one another. And when x and y are distinct, the fact that x and y are distinct is fully grounded in the fact that x stands in an irreflexive relation to y.

The objection is that there is a looming circularity in this proposal: we individuate objects in terms of weak discernibility, which is defined in terms of irreflexivity. Yet, the notion of an irreflexive relation seems to presuppose the notion of identity. Irreflexive relations, after all, are relations that objects cannot stand in *to themselves*. Clarifying the nature of this circularity is difficult; we must determine the sense in which an appeal to weak discernibility *presupposes* identity. Moreover, it is controversial whether this presupposition – if it exists – is problematic.

For the Weak Discernibility Proposal to distinguish between Castor and Pollux, it is important that Castor and Pollux do not have the same position or location. The fact that the spheres reside five meters apart provides an irreflexive relation, *five meters away*, that the Weak Discernibility Proposal uses to distinguish the objects. However, there are other cases where we may have qualitatively indiscernible yet distinct objects that cannot be distinguished by their positions.

The original Max Black cases are ones in which the spheres are spatially separated from each other. In the version of the example here, the spheres are five meters apart from each other. But French (1989) proposes a potential violation of the identity of indiscernibles involving objects that are not spatially separated from each other. French proposes that there are certain symmetrized states containing multiple subatomic particles (bosons) that cannot be distinguished by their positions. The bosons are allegedly qualitatively indiscernible.

This case, which I will call the "French Bosons" case is significant for multiple reasons. First, it challenges the Weak Discernibility Proposal. The proponent of the Weak Discernibility Proposal must specify which irreflexive relations the bosons stand in if not spatiotemporal distance relations. Second, the French Bosons case is an example taken from our physical theories. This means that *actual* conditions may provide a counterexample to the identity of indiscernibles. Thus, the French Bosons case threatens material, modal, and explanatory versions of the identity of indiscernibles.

Supporters of the Weak Discernibility Proposal have responded to the French Bosons case. Saunders (2006) claims that the bosons in the symmetrized state do not stand in any irreflexive relations, and on this basis, we should reject the claim that the bosons count as objects at all. Other responses on behalf of the Weak Discernibility Proposal suggest that the bosons stand in certain irreflexive relations, but the existence of these relations is controversial.[60]

---

[60] See Saunders and Muller (2008), Muller and Seevinck (2009), Caulton and Butterfield (2012), Huggett and Norton (2014), and French (2015) for a discussion of alternative methods for distinguishing subatomic particles.

4.3.2 The Parthood Proposal

The Weak Discernibility Proposal is only one option for providing an alternative principle of object individuation. We may also try to distinguish objects based on their parts. This proposal is that objects x and y are identical if and only if x is part of y and y is part of x (see Burgess [2012]). We can formulate a material version of the Parthood Proposal as follows:

The Parthood Proposal: $\forall x \forall y (x = y = (x$ is part of y & y is part of $x))$[61]

If x is part of y and y is part of x, x is an improper part of y (and y is an improper part of x). We can understand improper parthood in terms of identity: x is an improper part of y just in case x is identical with y. However, while the proponent of the Parthood Proposal may accept this biconditional claim, they will likely resist *defining* improper parthood by appeal to identity given that they want to provide an identity criterion in terms of parthood. Instead, the proponent of the Parthood Proposal may leave the *is a part of* relation as primitive or undefined.

Improper parthood is contrasted with proper parthood. An object x is a proper part of y when x is part of y and y is distinct from x. For example, a branch is a proper part of a tree. Proper parthood is asymmetric: if x is a proper part of y, then y is not a proper part of x. Objects x and y are distinct if x is a proper part of y or y is a proper part of x. Objects x and y will also be distinct if neither is a proper or improper part of the other.

The Parthood Proposal easily distinguishes everyday concrete objects. The Empire State Building is distinct from the Prado: neither is a part of the other. A horse is distinct from its leg: while the leg is part of the horse, the horse is not part of its own leg. The Parthood Proposal also seems to capture the correct result in the Max Black and French Bosons cases. Neither Castor nor Pollux is a part of the other. And the proponent of the Parthood Proposal can claim that neither boson is part of the other.

The Parthood Proposal has limitations. It seemingly can only distinguish concrete objects (under the assumption that abstracta do not have parts). Additionally, the Parthood Proposal may offer a *definition* of identity in terms of parthood, and some will resist defining identity in terms of parthood. Sider articulates this resistance:

> [C]onsider the objection that adopting parthood in fundamental theories allows the elimination of identity from ideology via the definition '$x = y =$ df x is part of y and y is part of x'. The savings in ideological parsimony would

---

be outweighed by increased complexity in the laws, which I take to include laws of logic and metaphysics. The logical laws governing '=' must now be rewritten in terms of the proposed definition, making them more complex; and further, the laws of mereology will be needed. (Sider 2013: n. 10)

Sider believes that if we take identity to be defined in terms of part, then parthood should count as more fundamental than identity. But if we replace the notion of "identity" in the laws of logic and metaphysics with the more fundamental notion of "parthood," Sider believes that the laws will lose some of their simplicity. And simplicity is a theoretical virtue. We would also need to bloat our fundamental base with the presumed fundamental laws of mereology. Thus, the Parthood Proposal may not be the most attractive option for those who value parsimony.

Because the last two proposals we will consider have been proposed in the context of discussions of ground,[62] I will rely on explanatory versions of the proposals.

4.3.3 The Existence Proposal

When considering identity facts, one thought is that the identity and distinctness of objects is settled by their existence. To clarify, identity and distinctness facts hold in virtue of the existence of the objects in question. Burgess (2012: 90) states this view succinctly: identity facts "seem to be nothing over and above the relevant existential facts." Epstein (2015: 169–81) also entertains such a - proposal.[63] We can formulate an explanatory version of the Existence Proposal:

The Explanatory Existence Proposal:
If $x = y$, then $x = y$ is fully grounded in the fact that x exists.

and

If $x \neq y$, then $x \neq y$ is fully grounded in the plurality of facts: x exists, y exists

The identity fact Hesperus = Phosphorous is fully grounded in the fact that Hesperus exists. The distinctness fact the Louvre $\neq$ the Prado is fully grounded in the plurality of facts: the Louvre exists, the Prado exists. The Existence Proposal can also accommodate the Max Black case, or so its proponents would claim. The distinctness of Castor and Pollux is explained, but it's not explained by a difference in the spheres' properties. The distinctness of Castor and Pollux is explained by the plurality of facts: Castor exists, Pollux exists. Likewise, the

---

[62] See Burgess (2012) and Shumener (2020a, 2020b).
[63] See Wilhelm (2020) for discussion as well.

fact that boson a is distinct from boson b in the symmetrized state is explained by the plurality of existence facts: boson a exists, boson b exists.

Burgess highlights a difficulty for the Explanatory Existence Proposal: The proponent cannot take an existence fact such as, b exists, to have the standard form $\exists x(x = b)$ without facing a looming circularity objection. If $b = b$ is grounded in $\exists x(x = b)$ and the existential generalization is fully grounded in its instances, then $\exists x(x = b)$ is fully grounded in $b = b$. And if ground is transitive, then $b = b$ will be grounded in $b = b$. This is problematic because we are searching for an explanation of identity and distinctness facts, and explanations should not violate irreflexivity. There are multiple avenues of response open to the proponent of the Explanatory Existence Proposal. They can deny the transitivity of ground, they can deny that existential generalizations are grounded in their instances, or they can deny that existence facts always take the form of existential generalizations.[64]

4.3.4 The Zero-Grounding Proposal

The final alternative to the identity of indiscernibles we will consider is the Zero-Grounding Proposal.

The Zero-Grounding Proposal takes identity facts to be zero-grounded. This option has been explored by Fine (2012) and, in arithmetical contexts by Donaldson (2017) (see Litland [2017] as well for related discussion of zero-grounding). A fact is zero-grounded when it is not grounded in further facts, and it is not ungrounded either. A zero-grounded fact is generated but not by anything. Fine states the difference being ungrounded and being zero-grounded:

> There is a ... distinction to be drawn between being zero-grounded and ungrounded. In the one case, the truth in question simply disappears from the world, so to speak. What generates it ... is its zero-ground. But in the case of an ungrounded truth ... the truth is not even generated. (Fine 2012: 48)

Fine suggests taking identity facts to be zero-grounded:

> But in other cases – as with Socrates being identical to Socrates or with Socrates belonging to singleton Socrates – it is not so clear what the contingent truths might be; and a plausible alternative is to suppose that they are somehow grounded in nothing at all. (Fine 2012: 48)

---

[64] For discussion of these ideas, though not always in the context of grounding identity and distinctness facts, see works by Fine (2012), McSweeney (2020), Poggiolesi (2020), and Krämer (2020).

Thus, we would take facts like the White House = the White House and Hesperus = Phosphorous to be zero-grounded. While Fine and Donaldson only discuss zero-grounding identity facts, we can extend this proposal to distinctness facts. Shumener (2020b) formulates (but does not defend) an explanatory zero-grounding proposal for identity and distinctness facts.

The Explanatory Zero-Grounding Proposal:
> If $x = y$, then $x = y$ is zero-grounded
>
> and
>
> If $x \neq y$, then $x \neq y$ is zero-grounded

Can the Explanatory Zero-Grounding Proposal accommodate the Max Black and French Bosons examples? It is not clear. The proponent of this proposal would say that the facts Castor $\neq$ Pollux and boson a $\neq$ boson b are both zero-grounded: they are not fundamental, but they are also not grounded by further facts. This explanation of distinctness facts may not be compelling if, when explaining $x \neq y$, we aim to explain why $x \neq y$ rather than $x = y$. If both $x \neq y$ and $x = y$ are grounded or explained in the same way (by being zero-grounded), we do not have an explanation of why the distinctness fact holds rather than the identity fact.

4.4 No Criteria for Object Identity

A more radical reaction to the problems posed by the Max Black and French Bosons examples is to reject the need for criteria for object identity.[65] In Section 1, I noted that we may deny the existence of explanatory identity criteria if we take identity and distinctness facts to be primitive or ungrounded.

Fiocco (2021) also defends the proposal that the "individuation of a thing is inexplicable" (yet, it is not clear that he would deem identity and distinctness facts to be metaphysically fundamental in the sense of fundamentality invoked in grounding contexts). Fiocco believes that the identity or distinctness of objects serves as a "precondition" of their standing in other kinds of relations to each other. For instance, Castor and Pollux's being distinct may be a precondition of their being spatially separated from each other. Fiocco asserts that their serving as preconditions renders identity and distinctness facts inexplicable. If we accept that the individuation of objects is inexplicable, we will presumably deny the existence of explanatory identity criteria.

---

[65] See Merricks (1998) for a rejection of diachronic identity criteria, with a focus on identity criteria in the debate over personal identity.

Denying the existence of explanatory identity criteria does not automatically lead us to reject the existence of material and modal identity criteria. What specific reasons do we have to deny the existence of material and modal identity criteria? One reason to reject modal and material identity criteria arises if we deny the existence of the identity relation. This is an extreme suggestion: we often deploy the identity predicate, "="; it is a commonplace notion in our mathematical, logical, and metaphysical theories. Why should we believe that there is no identity relation corresponding to this predicate? We have already encountered a view that denies the existence of an absolute identity relation. Relative Identity theorists (Section 2) deny that there are identity facts of the form x = y because they only acknowledge the existence of relative identity relations, such as *same statue as* and *same lump as*. If we deny the existence of the absolute identity relation, then presumably, we will deny the existence of identity criteria involving this relation as well.

Another, even more extreme, reason to deny the existence of material and modal identity criteria emerges if one denies the existence of both absolute and relative identity relations.[66] Wittgenstein and Russell doubted the existence of the identity relation. In Russell's (1903: 63) words:

> The question whether identity is or is not a relation, and even whether there is such a concept at all, is not easy to answer. For, it may be said, identity cannot be a relation, since, where it is truly asserted, we have only one term, whereas two terms are required for a relation. And indeed identity, an objector may urge, cannot be anything at all: two terms plainly are not identical, and one term cannot be, for what is it identical with?

And Wittgenstein (1922: 5.5301) claimed in the *Tractatus*, "That identity is not a relation between objects is obvious." Were we to deny the existence of identity relations full stop, we could not formulate material and modal identity criteria in the ways we do in this Element. Perhaps we can reformulate identity criteria in terms of monadic identity properties, but it is not clear how that would work.

I am not certain that one must go to these lengths to reject the existence of material, modal, or explanatory identity criteria. Perhaps we can accept the existence of an absolute identity relation, yet still deny that there are informative, general identity criteria for objects. One idea is to take identity and distinctness facts involving objects to be brute and to claim that such identity and distinctness facts are not accompanied by any nontrivial identity criteria.

---

[66] See Wehmeier (2012) for a contemporary defense of this idea.

5 Concluding Remarks

This Element has explored three varieties of identity criteria: the material, the modal, and the explanatory. One aim has been to examine the differences among these types of identity criteria as well as the reasons in favor of adopting certain formulations over others.

Another aim of this element has been to tie together discussions of Leibniz's Law from somewhat disconnected debates in metaphysics, philosophy of science, and philosophy of language. I discussed Leibniz's Law and the puzzling phenomena surrounding the indiscernibility of identicals and the identity of indiscernibles. I examined the reasons for and against accepting Leibniz's Law with a focus on contemporary treatment of the topic. I also explored options for rejecting the two principles.

Many of the criteria for object identity proposed in the penultimate section of the Element have not yet been fully articulated or defended. There is room to explore and develop these (and alternative) positions. My hope is that the reader now understands these contemporary debates and is well-positioned to contribute to them.

References

Adams, M. M. (1976). "Ockham on Identity and Distinction." *Franciscan Studies* 36 (1):5–74.

Adams, R. M. (1979). "Primitive Thisness and Primitive Identity." *Journal of Philosophy* 76 (1):5–26.

Bacon, A. & Russell, J. S. (2019). "The Logic of Opacity." *Philosophy and Phenomenological Research* 99 (1):81–114.

Baker, L. R. (1997). "Why Constitution Is Not Identity." *Journal of Philosophy* 94 (12):599–621.

Baxter, D. L. M. (1988). "Many-One Identity." *Philosophical Papers* 17 (3):193–216.

(2018). "Self-Differing, Aspects, and Leibniz's Law." *Noûs* 52:900–20.

Bennett, K. (2004). "Spatio-Temporal Coincidence and the Grounding Problem." *Philosophical Studies* 118 (3):339–71.

Black, M. (1952). "The Identity of Indiscernibles." *Mind* 61 (242):153–64.

Boolos, G. (1997). "Is Hume's Principle Analytic?" In R. G. Heck (ed.), *Language, Thought, and Logic: Essays in Honour of Michael Dummett*. Oxford University Press. pp. 245–62.

Bricker, P. (2008). "Concrete Possible Worlds." In T. Sider, J. Hawthorne & D. W.Zimmerman (eds.), *Contemporary Debates in Metaphysics*. Blackwell. pp. 111–34.

(2021). "Composition as Identity, Leibniz's Law, and Slice-Sensitive Emergent Properties." *Synthese*: 4389–409.

Bueno, O. (2014). Why Identity Is Fundamental. *American Philosophical Quarterly* 51 (4):325–32.

Burgess, A. (2012). "A Puzzle about Identity." *Thought: A Journal of Philosophy* 1 (2):90–99.

Caie, M., Goodman, J., & Lederman, H. (2020). "Classical Opacity." *Philosophy and Phenomenological Research* 101 (3):524–66.

Caplan, B. & Muller, C. (2015). "Brutal Identity." In S. Brook & A. Everett (eds.), *Fictional Objects*. Oxford University Press. pp. 174–207.

Carmichael, C. (2016). Deep Platonism. *Philosophy and Phenomenological Research* 92 (2):307–28.

Caulton, A. & Butterfield, J. (2012). "On Kinds of Indiscernibility in Logic and Metaphysics." *British Journal for the Philosophy of Science* 63 (1):27–84.

Cotnoir, A. J. (2013). "Composition as General Identity." In K. Bennett & D. W. Zimmerman (eds.), *Oxford Studies in Metaphysics*. Oxford University Press. pp. 294–322.

Cotnoir, A. J. & Baxter, D. L. M. (eds.) (2014). *Composition as Identity*. Oxford University Press.

Cowling, S. (2015). "Non-qualitative Properties." *Erkenntnis* 80 (2):275–301.

Curley, E. M. (1971). "Did Leibniz State 'Leibniz' Law'?" *Philosophical Review* 80 (4):497–501.

Della Rocca, M. (2005). "Two Spheres, Twenty Spheres, and the Identity of Indiscernibles." *Pacific Philosophical Quarterly* 86:480–92.

deRosset, L. (2013). What Is Weak Ground? *Essays in Philosophy* 14 (1):7–18.

Descartes, R. (1984 [1641]). *Meditations on First Philosophy*. Caravan Books.

Deutsch, H. & Garbacz, P. (2008). "Relative Identity." In E. N. Zalta (ed.), *Stanford Encyclopedia of Philosophy*. https://plato.stanford.edu/entries/identity-relative.

Doepke, F. C. (1982). "Spatially Coinciding Objects." *Ratio* 24:45–60.

Donaldson, T. (2017). "The (Metaphysical) Foundations of Arithmetic?" *Noûs* 51 (4):775–801.

Dorr, C. (2014). "Transparency and the Context-Sensitivity of Attitude Reports." In M. García-Carpintero & G. Martí (eds.), *Empty Representations: Reference and Non-Existence*. Oxford University Press. pp. 25–66.

   (2019). "Natural Properties." In E. N. Zalta (ed.), *Stanford Encyclopedia of Philosophy*. https://plato.stanford.edu/entries/natural-properties.

Eddon, M. (2010). Three Arguments from Temporary Intrinsics. *Philosophy and Phenomenological Research* 81 (3):605–19.

   (2011). "Intrinsicality and Hyperintensionality." *Philosophy and Phenomenological Research* 82 (2):314–36.

Epstein, B. (2015). *The Ant Trap: Rebuilding the Foundations of the Social Sciences*. Oxford University Press.

Feldman, F. (1970). Leibniz and "Leibniz' Law." *Philosophical Review* 79 (4):510–22.

Fine, K. (1983). "A Defence of Arbitrary Objects." *Proceedings of the Aristotelian Society, Supplementary Volume* 57:55–77.

   (1985a). "Natural Deduction and Arbitrary Objects." *Journal of Philosophical Logic* 14:57–107.

   (1985b). *Reasoning with Arbitrary Objects*. Blackwell.

   (2001). "The Question of Realism." *Philosopher's Imprint*, 1 (2):1–30.

   (2003). "The Non-identity of a Material Thing and Its Matter." *Mind* 112 (446):195–234.

   (2012). "A Guide to Ground." In F. Correia & B. Schnieder (eds.), *Metaphysical Grounding*. Cambridge University Press. pp. 37–80.

   (2016). "Identity Criteria and Ground." *Philosophical Studies*, 173 (1):1–19.

Fiocco, M. O. (2021). "There Is Nothing to Identity." *Synthese* 199 (3–4):7321–37.

Frege, G. (1879). *Begriffsschrift, eine der arithmetischen nachgebildete Formelsprache des reinen Denkens*. Louis Nebert.

(1892). "Über Sinn und Bedeutung." *Zeitschrift für Philosophie Und Philosophische Kritik* 100 (1):25–50.

(1980 [1884]). *The Foundations of Arithmetic: A Logico-mathematical Enquiry into the Concept of Number* [*Die Grundlagen der Arithmetik: eine logisch mathematische Untersuchung über den Begriff der Zahl*], trans. J. L. Austin, 2nd rev. ed. Northwestern University Press.

(2013 [1893]). *Gottlob Frege: Basic Laws of Arithmetic* [*Grundgesetze der Arithmetik*], trans. and ed. P. A. Ebert & M. Rossberg. Oxford University Press.

French, S. (1989). "Why the Principle of the Identity of Indiscernibles Is Not Contingently True Either." *Synthese* 78 (2):141–66.

(2015). "Identity and Individuality in Quantum Theory." In E. N. Zalta (ed.), *Stanford Encyclopedia of Philosophy*. https://plato.stanford.edu/entries/qt-idind/.

French, S. & Krause, D. (2006). *Identity in Physics: A Historical, Philosophical, and Formal Analysis*. Oxford University Press.

Gallois, A. (2016). *The Metaphysics of Identity*. Routledge.

Garland, C. (2020). "Grief and Composition as Identity." *Philosophical Quarterly* 70 (280):464–79.

Geach, P. T. (1967). "Identity." *Review of Metaphysics* 21 (1):3–12.

(1973). "Ontological Relativity and Relative Identity." In M. K. Munitz (ed.), *Logic and Ontology*. New York University Press. pp. 287–302.

Glazier, M. (2020). "Explanation." In Michael J. Raven (ed.), *Routledge Handbook of Metaphysical Grounding*. Routledge. pp. 121–32.

Goodman, J. "Consequences of Conditional Excluded Middle." Unpublished manuscript. https://jeremy-goodman.com/ConsequencesCEM.pdf.

Hacking, I. (1975). "The Identity of Indiscernibles." *Journal of Philosophy* 72 (9):249–56.

Haslanger, S. (1989). Endurance and Temporary Intrinsics. *Analysis* 49 (3):119–25.

Hawley, K. (2001). *How Things Persist*. Oxford University Press.

(2006). "Weak Discernibility." *Analysis* 66 (4):300–3.

(2009). "Identity and Indiscernibility." *Mind* 118 (469):101–19.

Hawthorne, J. (2003). "Identity." In M. J. Loux & D. W. Zimmerman (eds.), *The Oxford Handbook of Metaphysics*. Oxford University Press. pp. 99–130.

Heck, R. (1997). "The Julius Caesar Objection." In R. G. Heck (ed.), *Language, Thought, and Logic: Essays in Honour of Michael Dummett*. Oxford University Press. pp. 273–308.

Heller, M. (1990). *The Ontology of Physical Objects: Four-Dimensional Hunks of Matter*. Cambridge University Press.

Hoffmann-Kolss, V. (2019). "Defining Qualitative Properties." *Erkenntnis* 84 (5):995–1010.

Horsten, L. (2019). *The Metaphysics and Mathematics of Arbitrary Objects*. Cambridge University Press.

Huggett, N. & Norton, J. (2014). "Weak Discernibility for Quanta, the Right Way." *British Journal for the Philosophy of Science* 65 (1):39–58.

Hume, D. (2007). *A Treatise of Human Nature: Volume 1*, ed. M. Norton & J. Norton. Clarendon Press.

Hume, D. & Macnabb, D. G. C. (eds.) (1738). *A Treatise of Human Nature: Being an Attempt to Introduce the Experimental Method of Reasoning Into Moral Subjects*. Collins.

Jauernig, A. (2008). "The Modal Strength of Leibniz's Principle of the Identity of Indiscernibles." *Oxford Studies in Early Modern Philosophy* 4:191–225.

Johnston, M. (1992). "Constitution Is Not Identity." *Mind* 101 (401):89–106.

Klev, A. (2017). "Identity and Sortals." *Erkenntnis* 82 (1):1–16.

Koslicki, K. (2004). "Constitution and Similarity". *Philosophical Studies* 117 (3):327–63.

  (2015). "The Coarse-Grainedness of Grounding." In K. Bennett & D. W. Zimmerman (eds.), *Oxford Studies in Metaphysics*, vol. 9. Oxford University Press. pp. 306–42.

Krämer, S. (2020). "The Logical Puzzles of Ground." In M. J. Raven (ed.), *Routledge Handbook of Metaphysical Grounding*. Routledge. pp. 413–24.

Kripke, S. A. (1980). *Naming and Necessity: Lectures Given to the Princeton University Philosophy Colloquium*. Harvard University Press.

  (2005). "Russell's Notion of Scope." *Mind* 114 (456):1005–37.

Langton, R. & Lewis, D. K. (1998). "Defining 'Intrinsic'." *Philosophy and Phenomenological Research* 58 (2):333–45.

Leibniz, G. W. (1973 [1696]). "On the Principle of Indiscernibles." In *Philosophical Writings*, ed. G. H. R. Parkinson, trans. M. Morris & G. H. R. Parkinson. J. M. Dent and Sons Ltd. pp. 133–35.

  (1996). *New Essays on Human Understanding*, trans. and ed. P. Remnant and J. Bennett. Cambridge University Press.

Lewis, D. K. (1983). "New Work for a Theory of Universals." *Australasian Journal of Philosophy* 61 (4):343–77.

Lewis, D. K. (1986). *On the Plurality of Worlds*. Blackwell Publishers.

Lewis, E. (1995). "The Stoics on Identity and Individuation." *Phronesis* 40 (1):89–108.

Linnebo, Ø. (2005). "To Be Is to Be an F." *Dialectica* 59 (2):201–22.

Litland, J. (2017). "Grounding Grounding." *Oxford Studies in Metaphysics* 10: 279–316.

Locke, J. (1979 [1689]). *An Essay Concerning Human Understanding*, ed. P. Nidditch, rev. ed. Oxford University Press.

Lowe, E. J. (1989). "What Is a Criterion of Identity?" *Philosophical Quarterly* 39 (154):1–21.

(1995). "Coinciding Objects: In Defence of the 'Standard Account'." *Analysis* 55 (3):171–78.

Magidor, O. (2011). "Arguments by Leibniz's Law in Metaphysics." *Philosophy Compass* 6 (3):180–95.

Maurin, A.-S. (2019). "Grounding and Metaphysical Explanation: It's Complicated." *Philosophical Studies* 176 (6):1573–94.

McDaniel, K. (2008). "Against Composition as Identity." *Analysis* 68 (2):128–33.

McSweeney, M. (2020). "Logic." In Michael J. Raven (ed.), *The Routledge Handbook of Metaphysical Grounding*. Routledge. pp. 449–59.

Merricks, T. (1998). "There Are No Criteria of Identity Over Time." *Noûs* 32 (1):106–24.

Mooney, J. (2022). "Criteria of Identity Without Sortals." *Noûs* 00:1–18 https://doi.org/10.1111/nous.12419.

Muller, F. A. & Seevinck, M. P. (2009). "Discerning Elementary Particles." *Philosophy of Science* 76 (2):179–200.

Nelson, M. (2019) "Propositional Attitude Reports." In E. N. Zalta (ed.), *Stanford Encyclopedia of Philosophy*. https://plato.stanford.edu/entries/prop-attitude-reports.

O'Leary-Hawthorne, J. (1995). "The Bundle Theory of Substance and the Identity of Indiscernibles." *Analysis* 55 (3):191–96.

Parfit, D. (1971). "Personal Identity." *Philosophical Review* 80 (January):3–27.

Plate, J. (in press). "Qualitative Properties and Relations." *Philosophical Studies*: 1–26.

Parsons, C. (1965). "Frege's Theory of Numbers." In M. Black (ed.), *Philosophy in America*. Cornell University Press. pp. 180–203.

Paul, L. (2006). "Coincidence as Overlap." *Noûs* 40 (4):623–59.

Paul, L. (2010). "The Puzzles of Material Constitution." *Philosophy Compass* 5 (7):579–90.

Poggiolesi, F. (2020). "Logics of Ground." In Michael J. Raven (ed.), *Routledge Handbook of Metaphysical Grounding*. Routledge. pp. 413–24.

Quine, W. V. (1960). "Word and Object." *Les Etudes Philosophiques* 17 (2):278–79.

Quine, W. V. (1976). "Grades of Discriminability." *Journal of Philosophy* 73 (5):113–16.

Raven, M. J. (2013). "Is Ground a Strict Partial Order?" *American Philosophical Quarterly*, 50 (2):191–99.

(2015). "Ground." Philosophy Compass, 10 (5):322–33.

(2020) "Kit Fine." *The Internet Encyclopedia of Philosophy.* https://iep .utm.edu/fine-k/#:~:text=Kit%20Fine%20is%20an%20English,turn% 20within%20contemporary%20analytic%20philosophy.

Rodriguez-Pereyra, G. (2006). "How Not to Trivialise the Identity of Indiscernibles." In P. F. Strawson & A. Chakrabarti (eds.), *Concepts, Properties and Qualities*. Ashgate.

(2014). *Leibniz's Principle of Identity of Indiscernibles*. Oxford University Press.

(2017). "Indiscernible Universals." *Inquiry: An Interdisciplinary Journal of Philosophy* 60 (6):604–24.

Rosen, G. (2010). "Metaphysical Dependence: Grounding and Reduction." In B. Hale & A. Hoffman (eds.), *Modality: Metaphysics, Logic, and Epistemology*. Oxford University Press. pp. 109–36.

Russell, B. (1903). *The Principles of Mathematics*. Allen & Unwin.

Salmon, N. (2010). "Lambda in Sentences with Designators: An Ode to Complex Predication." *Journal of Philosophy* 107 (9):445–68.

Saunders, S. (2006). "Are Quantum Particles Objects?" *Analysis* 66 (1):52–63.

Saunders, S. & Muller, F. A. (2008). "Discerning Fermions." *British Journal for the Philosophy of Science* 59 (3):499–548.

Schaffer, J. (2009). "On What Grounds What." In D. Chalmers, D. Manley & R. Wasserman (eds.), *Metametaphysics: New Essays on the Foundations of Ontology*. Oxford University Press. pp. 347–83.

(2012). "Grounding, Transitivity, and Contrastivity." In F. Correia & B. Schnieder (eds.), *Metaphysical Grounding: Understanding the Structure of Reality*. Cambridge University Press. pp. 122–38.

Schiffer, S. "The Mode-of-Presentation Problem." In C. Anthony Anderson & J. Owens (eds.), *Propositional Attitudes: The Role of Content in Logic, Language, and Mind*. CSLI. pp. 249–68.

Shoemaker, S. (1999). "I–Sydney Shoemaker: Self, Body, and Coincidence." *Aristotelian Society Supplementary Volume* 73 (1):287–306.

Shumener, E. (2020a). "Explaining Identity and Distinctness." *Philosophical Studies* 177 (7):2073–96.

(2020b). "Identity." In M. J. Raven (ed.), *Routledge Handbook of Metaphysical Grounding*. Routledge. pp. 413–24.

Sider, T. (2001). *Four Dimensionalism: An Ontology of Persistence and Time*. Oxford University Press.

(2007). "Neo-fregeanism and Quantifier Variance." *Aristotelian Society Supplementary Volume* 81 (1):201–32.

(2013). "Against Parthood." *Oxford Studies in Metaphysics* 8:237–93.

Skiles, A. (2015). "Against Grounding Necessitarianism." *Erkenntnis* 80 (4):717–51.

Skow, B. (2007). "Are Shapes Intrinsic?" *Philosophical Studies* 133 (1):111–30.

Thomasson, A. L. (2014). *Ontology Made Easy.* Oxford University Press.

Thompson, N. (2016). "Grounding and Metaphysical Explanation." *Proceedings of the Aristotelian Society,* 116 (3):395–402

Thomson, J. J. (1983). "Parthood and Identity Across Time." *Journal of Philosophy* 80 (4):201–20.

(1998). "The Statue and the Clay." *Noûs* 32 (2):149–73.

Trogdon, K. (2013). "An Introduction to Grounding." In M. Hoeltje, B. Schnieder & A. Steinberg (eds.), *Varieties of Dependence.* Philosophia Verlag. pp. 97–122.

van Inwagen, P. (1994). "Composition as Identity." *Philosophical Perspectives* 8:207–20.

Wallace, M. (2011a). "Composition as Identity: Part 1." *Philosophy Compass* 6 (11):804–16.

Wallace, M. (2011b). "Composition as Identity: Part 2." *Philosophy Compass* 6 (11):817–27.

Wehmeier, K. F. (1967). *Identity and Spatio-Temporal Continuity.* Blackwell.

(2012). "How to Live Without Identity – And Why." *Australasian Journal of Philosophy* 90 (4):76–777.

Whiting, J. (1999). "Back to 'The Self and the Future'." *Philosophical Topics* 26 (1–2):441–77.

Wiggins, D. (2001). *Sameness and Substance Renewed.* Cambridge University Press.

(1967). *Identity and Spatio-temporal Continuity.* Blackwell.

Wilhelm, I. (2020). "An Argument for Entity Grounding." *Analysis* 80 (3):500–7.

(2021). "The Counteridentical Account of Explanatory Identities." *Journal of Philosophy* 118 (2):57–78.

Williams, B. (1970). "The Self and the Future." *Philosophical Review* 79 (2):161–80.

Williamson, T. (1990). *Identity and Discrimination,* vol. 42. Blackwell.

(2001). "Vagueness, Identity and Leibniz's Law." In P. Giaretta, A. Bottani & M. Carrara (eds.), *Individuals, Essence and Identity.* Kluwer Academic Publishers.

Wilson, J. (2014). "No Work for a Theory of Grounding." *Inquiry*, 57 (5–6):535–79.

Wittgenstein, L., Colombo, G. C. M., & Russell, Bertrand (1922). *Tractatus Logico-Philosophicus*. Fratelli Bocca.

Wörner, D. (2021). "On Making a Difference: Towards a Minimally Non-Trivial Version of the Identity of Indiscernibles." *Philosophical Studies* 178 (12):4261–78.

Wright, C. (1983). *Frege's Conception of Numbers as Objects*. Aberdeen University Press.

Wright, C. & Hale, B. (2001). *The Reason's Proper Study: Essays Towards a Neo-Fregean Philosophy of Mathematics*. Clarendon Press.

Yablo, S. (1987). "Identity, Essence, and Indiscernibility." *Journal of Philosophy* 84 (6):293–314.

Cambridge Elements ☰

Metaphysics

Tuomas E. Tahko

University of Bristol

Tuomas E. Tahko is Professor of Metaphysics of Science at the University of Bristol, UK. Tahko specializes in contemporary analytic metaphysics, with an emphasis on methodological and epistemic issues: 'meta-metaphysics'. He also works at the interface of metaphysics and philosophy of science: 'metaphysics of science'. Tahko is the author of *Unity of Science* (Cambridge University Press, 2021, Elements in Philosophy of Science), *An Introduction to Metametaphysics* (Cambridge University Press, 2015), and editor of *Contemporary Aristotelian Metaphysics* (Cambridge University Press, 2012).

About the Series

This highly accessible series of Elements provides brief but comprehensive introductions to the most central topics in metaphysics. Many of the Elements also go into considerable depth, so the series will appeal to both students and academics. Some Elements bridge the gaps between metaphysics, philosophy of science, and epistemology.

Cambridge Elements ☰

Metaphysics

Elements in the Series

Relations
John Heil

Material Objects
Thomas Sattig

Time
Heather Dyke

Metaphysical Realism and Anti-Realism
JTM Miller

Properties
Anna-Sofia Maurin

Persistence
Kristie Miller

Identity
Erica Shumener

A full series listing is available at: www.cambridge.org/EMPH

Printed in the United States
by Baker & Taylor Publisher Services